THE MYSTERY OF CHRIST
THE BIBLE DECODED
VOLUME TWO

NEVILLE GODDARD

ALIO PUBLISHING GROUP

paperback ISBN: 14.99 978-1-961959-12-5

ebook ISBN: 978-1-961959-11-8

hardover ISBN: 978-1-961959-13-2

https://www.aliopublishing.com

CONTENTS

PREFACE

"So, this comes to us — this mystery called "Christ". He comes to us as one unknown, but not from the outside. He is on the inside. He rises in us as "one unknown," in the most strange, wonderful, and ineffable way. He is That One who lets us experience Who-He-Is." – Neville

It is December 2023 as of this writing, and the mystery of Christ continues to reign as one of the world's greatest. The questions have remained mostly consistent over millennia:

"Was he real?"

"What did he look like?"

"Was he really the Son of God?"

"Did a man named Jesus die on the cross?"

...and so on.

The late Neville Goddard, one of the most prominent and influential thinkers and teachers of the New Thought movement, had a unique and, to some, controversial perspective on The Anointed One. Here, in *The Mystery of Christ*, I invite you, dear reader, to explore this great and enduring enigma from highly nuanced and detailed angles, with fresh eyes and an open mind...as well as a desire to know for your self what is, and isn't, real.

Further on you will find a series of lectures Neville Goddard gave on the subject in the mid-20th century. His words have been preserved as much as possible, with minimal revisions only for the sake of increasing comprehension levels for the modern individual. That being said, there may still be instances where a re-read may be required for full retention of the material.

Essentially, this book serves as an opportunity for you – dear reader & courageous seeker – to grow, by feeding the roots of your own faith. And as the story (and message) of Christ is not exclusive to Christians (besides: did not Christ precede Christianity?), I humbly invite everyone with a free, thinking mind to explore these concepts and topics, no matter their religious background; or lack thereof.

In the words of Neville himself:

"Could you now dream of being the man or woman you want to be? That dream is a promise. We are told he was not swerved by anything in the world and gave all the glory to God, or imagining: fully convinced that God could do what He had promised."

May we all continue to blossom and mature in our understanding of this great mystery, for the sake of a greater mutual life as we live together on Earth. Thank you for reading, and all the best.

CHAPTER 1

GOOD FRIDAY

You know the story of Good Friday. A man is in a garden. It's night time. And one called Judas comes in search of him, seemingly to betray him. He comes into the garden, and it's dark, so he asks the simple question: "Where is Jesus?" Then the voice in the dark answered: "I AM HE."

We are told in the story that they all fell to the ground. When they regained their composure, they asked the same question: "Where is Jesus?" Again the voice answered: "I have told you that I AM HE." This time Judas kisses him and the voice said to him: "Now that you have found me, let all else go; but do not let Me go...and what you have to do, do quickly." Then Judas goes out and commits suicide.

Now when you read the story you might think that that drama took place in a garden. No. That drama MUST take place in the mind of man. For this is all about rebirth. It takes a man, a normal man, a man of sense; but hidden in that man and bound hand and foot is the second man that rebirth loosens and lifts up; and that second man is God.

So the mystery is all self, and he uses the word "mystery" no less than 18 times. He asked those in the Corinthians to esteem him as a steward of mystery. Then he said: "Great is the mystery; God was manifest in the flesh." Then he spoke of the greatest of all mysteries, the one hidden from the foundation of the world: "Christ in you is the hope of glory."

Christ IN man. Not Christ in the pages of history, but God IN man must be awakened – and this is the technique by which he is awakened. Now come closely with me and let me take you into the garden of your own mind.

Right now, just imagine you are in a sick room of some wonderful hospital; a ward. You see the case history.

You heard the verdict of the doctor, and the man, seemingly, is dying. What would save that man from such a verdict? What would save him? A state of health by which he would rise from that bed and become a normal, healthy person in this world; *that* would save him.

Now, look into your mind's eye, and carefully define the solution of a particular problem. When you define the solution to the problem, do you know what you are actually seeing? You are seeing Jesus, for Jesus means "to save." So the state that would save that man from what he is, is the state of health. *That* is his savior.

The story is, "Now that you have found ME, let all else go, but do not let ME go." In other words, let go of everything you have ever believed, but do not let go of this concept – that the man is well in spite of the evidence of your senses to the contrary. No matter what reason dictates, you hold onto Jesus, Jesus being that the man is healthy. You hold onto it, and you touch it by becoming intensely aware of it; that's the only way to touch a thing.

Let me tell you of something that happened only last Friday. I have a friend in this City who I met recently and he gave me a very sad story. He was up against it. He had borrowed money, and he can't pay it back. Things are just going from bad to worse. While shaving...you don't have to go into some church to find Him.

While shaving, I thought of him and I instantly, while in the act of shaving, imagined I was speaking to my wife, and I said to her, "Isn't it wonderful, the good news concerning George." Then I allowed her, in my imagination, to say, "Yes, isn't it wonderful."

Three hours later, he called me to tell me it's so good he doesn't know what, really, to take. He said that in the immediate present two, wonderful jobs are offered to him. Jobs he can do and do well. Both are great and he doesn't know which one to take. Now he has another problem.

I will now assume that he has taken the right one, the best one, and I know that in the immediate future, George will again call me and tell me that, on reflection, he could not have chosen more wisely. So, you look into your own mind's eye and know exactly what you want in this world. When you know what you want in place of what you are, then you are seeing your savior, your Jesus.

The story is, don't let Him go, but let all else go. Disengage yourself from the whole vast belief that you formerly entertained, and hold on in your imagination to the concept that you ARE the man that you want to be. That will lead you toward Calvary.

Calvary means fixing in your own mind's eye that state, and that will lead towards Easter or this wonderful day that we speak of as the Resurrection. For you will resurrect and make alive the state that began only as a concept. If you remain faithful to the concept you will be led right into the fulfillment of that state. It is called, in the Bible, re-birth.

Now here is the story. He said, "Except you be born again, you cannot enter the kingdom of heaven." The wise man said, "How is it possible a man my age may once again enter my mother's womb and be born again?" He said, "You, a master of Israel and you do not know? Except you be born of water and the spirit, ye can in no wise enter the kingdom of heaven."

Then he gives this clue, "As Moses lifted up the serpent in the wilderness, even so must the son of man be lifted up." ...As Moses lifted up the serpent... do you think a man lifted up a brazen serpent as told in the story and that everyone who looked on it was instantly healed and those who would not look were not cured? It's not any serpent.

A serpent is a symbol of the power of endless self-reproduction. For the serpent sheds its skin, and yet does not die. Man must be like the serpent, who grows and outgrows. So I must now learn the art of dying that I may live, rather than, I would say killing that I may survive. I die, by laying down all that I now believe, and I lift myself up to the belief that I am what I want to be. That's how I do it.

Now this is how a man is born of water and of the spirit. If I told you now that an assumption, though false, if persisted in, will harden into fact, that is a truth, that is water. But water is not enough. You must catch the spirit of it and apply that truth.

Well, if I know that if I assume that I am the man I want to be and persist in that assumption, I would gradually become that. If I have that knowledge, that's marvelous. But not to DO it is to try to bring this being to birth by water only.

We are told this is the one who came by water and the blood. Not by water only, but by water and the blood. In other words, I have the knowledge, but I cannot bring to birth my ideal by bare knowledge. I must put it into action, I must DO it. Then when I DO it, I take my savior and I crystallize him by the doing. This is the story of our wonderful Easter.

Today, our churches are bursting with new finery, but not bursting with new men, and we are told in the story, "Put on the Lord Jesus Christ. Put on the New Man." Well, how will I put on a New Man? It's like saying to the boy, put on manhood, or saying to the tree, put on foliage.

It comes from within, out and man puts it on from the outside. You can't put it on from the outside, for He is within you. For great is the mystery. The one hidden from the foundation of the earth, Christ in YOU is the hope of glory. Not some Christ external to yourself, but the one in you, that is your hope; that is your only glory.

So, the great mystery is that at Bethlehem God became as we are that at Calvary we may become as He is. And Calvary is the opportunity that comes very day in the life of a man. When you walk the earth and you see anyone in need, ask yourself what would be the solution to that individual's problem, just what would it be? You can grant it.

If you know who you REALLY are, you can grant it, just as I granted it to George. I didn't raise one finger to get George a job. I didn't send him on a job; I didn't give him anything. I simply turned in my own mind's eye to my wife, who was not physically present, and simply stated, "Isn't it wonderful, the news concerning George," and I allowed her to say, in my imagination, "Yes, isn't it wonderful," and then I continued with my project of a simple shaving.

That is simply lifting up the serpent in the wilderness. For I raised myself from the knowledge that George was unemployed and struggling to the knowledge that he is employed. I did nothing more. I shed the skin, like a serpent. I dropped off all that I formerly believed concerning George, and began to LIVE on a higher level concerning George, and I so lived it and so made it real that in three hours, he called and gave me this exciting news.

You can do the same thing with anything in this world. When you do it daily, you die daily as the prophet said, "I die daily." Man waits for some little event called death, and he thinks that is dying. That isn't really dying for the simple reason that that kind of death does not bring about a transformation. For there is no transformation in a physical death, but there is transformation in mentally dying and dying daily.

So, if you have learned the art of dying, you have learned the art of living. For man is immortal and he must die endlessly. For life was a creative idea, and it will find itself only in changing form.

If I do not change and grow and outgrow, and grow and outgrow, then I know nothing of the mystery of Easter, for Easter is really the greatest of all mysteries. It's when man awakens within himself from his birth at Bethlehem and he awakens as God. That's the story of Easter.

So, let us not perpetuate this thing by our finery, which is lovely. There is not a thing wrong with getting new clothes and new hats and all the lovely things in the world, but today it has become almost a parade of what is new rather than the new man.

So, when I put on the new man, I put him on by daily exercising him in this way. By becoming intensely aware. You could at this very moment, extend your feelings and trust your touch and participate in all the flights of your imagination, and do not be afraid of your sensitivities.

When I become intensely aware that I am hearing what I want to hear and am actually touching what I want to touch, virtue goes out of me, and the thing touched takes on the blessing which was determined by the mood that possessed me as I imagined that I touched it. If I now touch anything, it must become crystallized in my world, bearing witness to the mood that possessed me at the moment that I touched it.

So, unless we be born of this knowledge and the application of this knowledge, we cannot enter this eternal state called the Kingdom of Heaven. So, now you have a little of the knowledge, go out and apply it. When you apply it, this is what happens, and this is a mystical fact.

It was said of this one called Judah, "Who is this one who comes with his garments dyed in the sap of wine. Who takes his vestige and bathes it in the blood of grapes and takes his colt and ties it to a choice vine, and his eye red with wine, and his teeth white with milk?"

You are told in the very last act, "They placed a wine-colored robe upon Jesus." You are told that Judah took his robe and bathed it in the blood of grapes. Now when I took what I did for George, I was actually weaving my wine-colored robe. I must weave that robe if I would awaken.

It's called, in the Bible, the wedding garment. It is called the wine-colored robe. It is called the amethyst in the New Testament, the amethyst in the Old Testament. It's not an amethyst. It's not a robe I weave on the outside, but when I live a life according to these truths, I am actually weaving a wine-colored aura around my being which then enables me to function consciously on higher levels of my own being.

Without such a robe, I cannot function beyond my present physical state. But when I live this life according to these truths, you can't see it with the physical eye, but I weave my robe and those who have the eye opened will see me as one of their own, and I'm not going to carry some little insignia to tell them who I am. I radiate who I am when they see my garment.

So, when we are told, "Judah comes and he takes his wonderful robe and he bathes it in the blood of grapes" it's not a man who takes off a robe, for the garment in the Bible is what a man wears mentally.

So, if I take my mind and I apply it, actually all day long but not confining it to one simple little thing as I did for George, but in the course of a day I have unnumbered opportunities to weave this wonderful robe by simply hearing good news for others.

If I hear only good for others and trust what I hear as though I heard it, I am actually taking my robe and bathing it in the blood of grapes. You wonder why he called himself the vine? He said, "I AM the vine and ye are the branches. Unless the branch be rooted in the vine, it has no life."

Well every man in the world is a branch, rooted in me, the vine, and he ends in me as I am rooted in and end in God. Now that can be said of every man in the world. While you look at me and can hear me, you too can say it. Although I have just made the claim, "you are rooted in me," you can claim that I am rooted in you and I end in you as you are rooted in and end in God. If you know it, then it is your duty to lift up every man in this world.

Not one must be discarded.

Everyone must be redeemed and your life is the process by which this redemption is brought to pass. Discard no man. Every man can be changed. And you have the power to change him by taking the man and seeing him as he seemingly is and then asking what he would like to be instead of what he seems to be.

When you know what he would like to be, then you imagine that he is that being already. Turn to a loved one and commune with the loved one concerning this man, just as though it were a fact. When you do it, trust it, touch it and believe it, and I will tell you that man will become the embodiment of what you have imagined him to be.

This is Easter, and Easter comes not once a year, Easter is a daily opportunity to simply die that you may live. For here it is said, "If any man would come after me, let him deny himself and take up his cross daily and follow me." Any man.

Well, how would I take up my cross and follow after this idea? First, I am told I must deny myself. Usually man thinks that means giving up something he loves, giving up the pleasures of the table, or giving up something of which he is especially fond. It hasn't a thing to do with giving up external things.

It is: a man must deny himself, and a man's true self is made up of the sum total of all that he believes, all that he accepts as true, all that he consents to. So, if I consent to a man dying, then I must deny that concept, that self, and put in its place the embodiment of a healthy being. When I do that, I can follow after this idea.

You can take this principle and apply it to everything in this world. If it's not some tangible thing on earth you want, take some noble concept of a man, take a man that you would love to see in this world. Dream of that man actually walking this earth and identify yourself with that man. Associate yourself in your own imagination with that as if you were he.

When you actually feel that I am he, and continue in that state, then things begin to unfold to bear witness to the truth of your assumption. You try it.

So, remember, Easter is the art of dying that you may live, and this reminds me of that wonderful poem of the death of Abdula and what he said at the end of it all. He appeared among all the mortals and they were weeping and kissing his worn-out body and he turned to them and said, "I am not the thing you kiss, cease your tears and let it lie. It was mine; it is not I."

CHAPTER 2

THE CRUCIFIXION

The crucifixion is the history of man. Our human history begins with birth, and ends with death. In Divine history...it begins with death, and ends with birth. There is a *complete reversal* of these histories.

Here we begin in the womb and end in the tomb...but in Divine history, we begin in the tomb and awaken in the womb, where we are born. Now here in this fantastic drama I think we have misconceived the part of Jesus Christ and made of him an idol, and having made him an idol he hides from us the true God.

Let us turn to the Book of Luke 18:31-34: "And taking the twelve he said to them 'Behold, we are going up to Jerusalem, and everything that is written of the Son of man by the prophets will be accomplished.

For he will be delivered to the Gentiles, and will be mocked and shamefully treated and spit upon; they will scourged him and kill him, and on the third day he will rise.' But they understood none of these things; this saying was hid from them, and they did not grasp what was said."

We are told that no one understood him. Now believe this; I am speaking to you, as I have tried every night, from experience.

I am not theorizing. I have no interest whatsoever in trying to set up some workable philosophy of life, I really haven't. If I made my exit tonight it would make no difference to me personally, maybe to my wife and my child, my family, - but not to me. This drama begins with the crucifixion.

"Unless I die thou canst not live;
But if I die I shall arise again and thou
    with me.
Wouldest thou die for one who never died
For thee, or ever die for one who had not
    died for thee."
(Blake Jer. Plate 96)

This is the story of every being born of woman. No child in the world could cross the threshold that admits to conscious life unaided by the death of God. It is God's purpose to give us himself as though there were no others in the world. Just God and you, God and I.

Believe this, really. If you believe it then the most unbelievable Gospel in the world becomes possible and believable; and it takes the son to reveal it to be true. Now this is the story as revealed to me.

You may think "well now that was only a dream. Wonderful, sure; exciting, yes – but still just a simple dream." May I tell you it was **not** a dream. It was an experience more vivid than this very moment. For true vision is far more alive than anything you have ever experienced in this world; *anything*.

This night in question I was walking with an enormous number as though the whole humanity walked in a certain direction; and I was one of the unnumbered. As I walked with them, I noted that they were all dressed in very colorful Middle Eastern attire; a voice shouted out of the blue, and it said: "And God walks with them."

A woman to my right, I would say in her thirties, maybe forty, a most attractive Arab; and she asked the voice: "If God walks with us where is he?" And the voice answered from the blue: "At your side." She took it as the whole vast world takes these things, - literally. And turning to her side she looked into my eyes and became hysterical, it struck her so funny. It was the funniest thing she had ever heard.

"God walks with us?" And she turned to a simple man with all of his frailties, all of his weaknesses, one she knew well; and having looked into his face, having heard the voice, - she said: "What! – Neville God?"

And the voice replied: "God laid himself down within you to sleep and as he slept he dreamed a dream, he dreamed" – and I completed the sentence: "He was dreaming he was me. How else would I be in this world if he didn't dream? And you awake from sheer emotionalism.

And may I tell you this is the sensation of the crucifixion. It's the most delightful sensation in the world; it is not painful. My hands became vortexes; my head a vortex; my feet vortexes; my side a vortex.

And here I was driven into this body on the bed through my emotionalism, held by six vortexes; my hand, my feet, my head and my side. And the delight, the sheer joy of being driven upon this cross, this body!

So I speak from experience; it is not a painful act. But it happened in the beginning of time. This was only a memory image returning; when I was about to awake. But in that interval, - how long, - who knows?

The Bible speaks of three days between the crucifixion and the resurrection; but that is all symbolism.

Blake calls it six thousand years. He said:

> "I behold the Visions of my deadly Sleep of
>   Six Thousand Years
> Dazzling around thy skirts like a Serpent of
>   precious stones and gold.
> I know it is my Self, O my Divine Creator
>   and Redeemer."
> (Jer. Plate 96)

Here we turn to the drama of this coming Friday all of Christian churches will re-enact; and they differ. Matthew 27:46 and Mark 15:34 gave the last cry on the cross as the quotation from Psalms 22:1 "My God, my God, why hast thou forsaken me?" John 19:20 gives it in the cry "It is finished."

Luke 23:46 substitutes the 31st Psalm, 5th verse for the 22nd Psalm: because he was using Mark's script. But he elaborates on Mark's script and he substituted Psalm 31:5 for Psalm 22:1, and this is what he quotes: "Father, into thy hands I commit my spirit!" This is the verse: "Into thy hand I commit my spirit; thou hast redeemed me, O Lord, faithful God." He kept his faith, for he told me:

"Unless I die thou canst not live; but if I
    die I shall arise again and thou
    with me."

There came the very act of crucifixion that was in itself resurrection. Yes, - an interval of time in between, no question about it. But may I tell you, no one in this world can fail. As quoted in Romans 6:5: "For if we have been united with Christ in a death like his, we shall certainly be united with him in a resurrection like his."

Everyone in this world will be resurrected; but it takes an interval of time with all the blows in the world to make the immortal garment. Now listen to this carefully. It has been given to me and you take it for what it is worth. The promise of this begins in Genesis 17:19, the promise of an infant called Isaac: and the whole vast world has the strangest concept of Isaac.

The Lord begat Isaac. Isaac is to be bought, not as the result of generation but the shaping of the begotten. Here is God the unbegotten shaping himself upon us; and when he completes that shape and it is perfect in his eyes then we are born from Above. So Isaac is the shaping of the unbegot, but God is not begotten, he is begetting himself on man, the individual man.

And when he begot himself in me to his satisfaction, I was born from Above and went through the entire series in the interval of nine months, - judged by Caesar's calendar. How many thousands of years prior to that I do not know, I cannot tell you. I would if I knew for I have no secrets; when I get it I tell you, but I do not know, the veil has not been lifted to that extent.

But I do know that when it pleased him, that which he begot in me, then it took nine months for the entire series of these mystical experiences as described in Scripture to completely unfold within me. So I can tell you it is going to happen to you. And so there's no time.

It took nine months from the moment of the Birth but when that Birth takes place it is all in God's keeping and you and I are put through the furnace of affliction. Let no one tell you that you are not going to, Isaiah 14:24: "As I have planned, so shall it be, as I have purposed, so shall it stand." And no one will thwart it, - but no one.

I am inclined to believe that in spite of the pain, in spite of all the things that man plots and plans in this world, there is a definite period. The Book of Habakkuk tells me it is, but they won't tell me what the period is. He says: "The vision has it's own appointed hour; it ripens, it will flower. If it be long then wait for it is sure, it will not be late."

If it will not be late and the vision has it's own appointed hour, well then, whether Blake is right or someone else is right, I do not know. But I assure you the last section takes only nine months, even though you linger for years beyond that nine months.

For you came into your inheritance at that third experience; but the glory of your heavenly inheritance cannot become actual, or is fully realized in the individual, so long as he is still in the body. The moment he takes off that veil, called the body, he is clothed in that garment that God, and God alone, made.

God was actually shaping himself upon this garment, without my consent, without my knowledge; molding that unbegotten Being that He is and giving me Himself. So when He succeeded in giving me Himself, it satisfied Him, that immortal garment that He would wear; so He wears it for his name is "I AM".

And may I tell you in all of my experiences I never had a change of identity, - never. I have always been aware of being "I am." I have never had any feeling of being other than who I am. And some thing was taking place in me, and it was God.

As we are told: Phil: 1:6: "He who began a good work in me will bring it to completion at the day of Jesus Christ."

Jesus Christ is a profession that is God and he will not stop it until he brings it to Jesus Christ in you. But we have taken Jesus Christ and made of him an image, an idol; and having made of him an idol he now hides from us the true God.

It is God, the only God, that is actually shaping himself upon you. And when that is shaped upon you, - this is a form, a mold, - but this cannot inherit the kingdom of heaven; this is flesh and blood. It takes this to mold it upon it, for what is being molded upon it is God, the unbegotten, and God being Spirit he is molding himself as spirit, the immortal you. And then you, God, are clothed.

Well, how could you clothe God in form? He is clothing himself in a shape and that is you, - so he begets us. But it began with the crucifixion. The crucifixion does not end the drama, it begins the drama. So every one becomes a breathing, living, conscious being because God died for him.

It's the mystery of life through death, as told us in John 12:24: "Unless a grain of wheat falls into the earth and dies, it remains alone; but if it dies, it bears much fruit." It has to fall into the earth and die, and this is the earth (the body) in God's kingdom. And God falls into this earth and dies, he forgets that He is God in His belief that He is man.

God actually becomes man that man may become God; and molds Himself; this Unbegotten Being upon man. And when He is satisfied with that molding process, it is in the eye of God that it's perfect; therefore, if it is perfect, then God is born in man.

So God actually gives Himself to us, to each of, as if there were no others in the world, - just God and you, God and I. Believe it. The whole story of the Gospel is this story.

So the crucifixion, from my own personal experience, is not as the churches depict it. The sorrow comes in between; that interval be it 6000 years, I do not know. But in that interval we have to be molded, as we are told in Isaiah 48:10,11: "I have tried you in the furnace of affliction. For my own sake, for my own sake, I do it."

For there is no other way in the world to bring me into that state of perfection and to weave me into an immortal body to receive God Himself as my own being. So I went through all the fires of affliction, and these fiery, fiery ordeals. So don't be concerned.

> "Whom God has afflicted for Secret Ends.
> He comforts and Heals and calls them
>   Friends."
> (Blake)

When you and I enter God's Golgotha, as we are told: "And when they came to the place which is called 'The skull', there they crucified him." (Luke 23:33) The word "skull", which is translated in the definition of Golgotha, - another definition is the "Holy Sepulcher". So now we know what the Holy Sepulcher is.

It is our own wonderful human skull, that's where he is crucified. But he is also nailed upon the cross. He is nailed through the feet and pierced on the side. Now here John gives so much time to the piercing of the side.

He does not give the cry of dereliction: "My God, my God, why hast thou forsaken me." John only claims: "It is finished" and then the soldiers shaft into the right side and out came blood and water. And down through the centuries they are trying in some way to explain it.

They can't explain it on anything that is biological, save that a birth always has the phenomena of blood and water. When a child is born the water is broken and there is a flowing of blood and water. This is birth.

To understand it we go back to the 31st Psalm: "Into thy hand I commit my spirit; thou hast redeemed me, O Lord, faithful God." He promised it and He did it. That is only a symbol of one's birth, which is redemption. So I say to you, don't weep when you see it, rejoice, it was God's sacrifice of himself because he desired to individualize himself in unnumbered garments, in all of us.

God can't beget anything other than God, so we are told in the 82nd Psalm: "God has taken his place in the divine council in the midst of the gods he holds judgment." On God in the midst of gods – all is God. He is asking and begetting this Unbegotten Being. The cue is given us in the Book of Hebrews 5:6. It is called by a different name, it is called Melchizedek.

He has no father, no mother, no genealogy. He is telling you who he is. Everyone who is Born from Above, - because God succeeded in giving Himself to that individual, - that individual has no genealogy. He is God the father. Believe me.

How could he give himself without knowing His son? I tell you the whole vast world of humanity is symbolized in a single youth, - called David. David is the whole world of humanity, in the language of symbolism. And the day will come in the second mystical experience in the nine month period, and here you look at David; and David is your son and you know it more surely then you know anything in the world.

There is no uncertainty when you look into his eyes and you see David and he calls you "My Lord, my father." You know for the first time who you really are. And you turn to the world and you tell them what happened. But you are told, as I quoted earlier from Luke 18:34: "They understood none of these things; this saying was hid from them, and they did not grasp what was said."

How can you persuade the individual that the day will come that even this very moment I could take the most orthodox Jew in the world, - if I went to Israel tonight, - and talked to the head Rabbi and asked him if he feels any relationship to David.

He would say: "Only as the greatest of the kings of Israel; but relationship as to myself, No." But he respects the great king of Israel, and hopes some day to rebuild the dynasty that is now gone. But he could not feel a relationship.

So if I, in his mind a total stranger – a gentile – would tell him I am his father he would spit in my face. To him that would be blasphemous; and yet I could tell him I am his father. I'll go further, I'll tell you, you are his father, and the day is coming it will be revealed to you. And when the whole vast world is completed and God's work is finished; and he has given himself to every being in the world...because he is the father of David.

To give me himself He has to give me fatherhood of David, - not just fatherhood. There is no need to give me fatherhood and not the father of his son. His son, yes. Psalm 2:7 "Thou art my son, today I have begotten thee." Then he takes this only begotten son to prove his gift to us by giving us that son as our son. And you look right into his eyes and he calls you "father," he calls you "Adonai, my lord."

I tell you the day will come when you and I will be the same father of the same child, everlasting eternal youth; that God in the beginning put into the mind of man and molded man into the likeness of himself. Read it in Eccl. 3:11. "God has put eternity into man's mind; yet so that he cannot find out what God has done from the beginning to the end."

The word translated "eternity" is the Hebrew word Olam. The Olam is translated, youth, lad, stripling. Listen to the words and see how we know who he is. The king wants to find out the identity of this fantastic youth that conquered the entire enemy of Israel, - he brings down the giant. So the king says to his lieutenant: "'Abner, whose son is that youth?'

And Abner said, 'As your soul lives, O king, I cannot tell.' And the king said, 'Inquire whose son the stripling is.'" No one knows. Now the stripling comes in with the head of the giant in his hands, the head of Goliath, the enemy of Israel. And the king said to him: "'Whose son are you, young man?' And David answered, 'I am the son of your servant Jesse, the Bethlehemite.'"

Now prophecy was made in I Samuel 17:2.5. "That the father of such a lad would be set free in Israel." Not the lad; the lad is buried in every being in the world. But the father of that lad, who knows he is the father, he is set free in heaven, free in the New Israel. So when one knows he is the father by actual experience; at that moment he is free in Israel.

The 6000 years of turmoil is over for him; but David is still to be redeemed, to be discovered in the minds of all. And everyone is going to find him, and finding him they will find the relationship of himself to that lad; and we all will be one and our name one when the curtain comes down on the final act of this marvelous play.

Blake said: "Do not let yourself be intimidated by the horror of the world. Everything is ordered and correct and must fulfill its destiny in order to attain perfection."

Everything is ordered, everything is perfect. God planned it just as it has come out and as he willed it, it will be consummated, and no tyrant in the world is going to stop it. He will take all the tyrants in the world and use them in the fulfillment of his purpose, as we are told in Proverbs 16:4: "The LORD has made everything for its purpose, even the wicked for the day of trouble."

Everything, not just a few. For it takes the wicked being to cross your path to add a little more fire to bring you closer into the image of God. If it takes many to cross it, they will cross your path. What man looking at this garment we are wearing now could ever see him in the image of God. But this is not what is molded; this is only a form on which he is molding himself.

When he has finished the molding then comes this fantastic experience in you; and you awake in a tomb. And the tomb all along was a womb; that was where you were crucified and you didn't know it. And one day you awake in a tomb and the tomb is your own wonderful skull; and that is the holy sepulcher.

This week thousands of pilgrims will go to Jerusalem, to the holy sepulcher. And some priests, quite innocently, will point out a place and say "That's it, that's where he was buried." He wasn't buried there at all. There is no holy place in Jerusalem.

The holy place is your own wonderful skull; that is the holy sepulcher, that is where he is buried. And that is where he is sound asleep dreaming with you these visions of eternity until you awake. When you awake you are he and he is your very own being.

It is his purpose to give you himself, and there is no way in eternity that God can give you himself and prove it, unless he also gives me his most precious possession in the world, - and that is his son. He doesn't give me his son to walk the street with me as a companion; he gives me his son as my son. So I look right into the eyes of the son of God and know him to be my son.

Then I wonder, how could this be? Here a man a few years old, weak, limited, with all the frailties of the world, all the weaknesses of the flesh, and yet, God so succeeded in his purpose for me, that he, the unbegotten gave me himself; therefore, I am unbegotten.

Though I seemingly had a beginning in time, with the gift of God, the unbegotten, I now cease to be begotten. I have no genealogy; I have no father, - I am father, - the father of his only begotten son. I tell you this is a mystery. But mysteries of this nature are not matters to be kept secret but truths that are mysterious in nature.

They are not things to be hidden. The minute they happen to you, you tell them to encourage every being in the world that in spite of the furnaces of the moment to continue, keep on moving, for you are moving anyway. But the end: - listen to the words: "O God, faithful Lord." He has kept his faith, he promised me in the beginning he would do it. "Thou hast redeemed me." And then sent me through furnaces without my consent, without my permission.

Take the story of Job. Here is one subjected to all the most horrible experiments in the world produced by God. And in the end he said (Job 42:5), "I heard of thee by the hearing of the ear, but now my eye sees thee." He sees the only thing in the world is reveal God to himself, because God is invisible to the world; but his son reveals God.

"No one knows who the Son is except the Father, or who the Father is except the Son, and any one to whom the Son chooses to reveal him." So, how will I ever know God? When his son comes in to my world and looks me in the face and calls me "father", then I know God.

And yet in spite of this may I tell you, the day will come you will still be taken into the presence of Infinite Love. And you don't have to ask who you are or anyone in the world who he is. As you stand in the presence of Infinite Love he embraces you; and you know who he is and who you are; for at that moment of the embrace you become one with the body of Infinite Love. Yes, that God is Almighty we know. But almightiness and omniscience are but aptitudes of God.

God himself is Love, absolute Love, and I can't describe it except to tell you it is man. When you look at him, Infinite Love, and he embraces you and you are lost in the body of God again, one with it, it is your body. And then he comes to the final journey. "And now I have told you before it takes place, so that when it does take place, you may believe." (John 14:29)

So I share with you my experience. Remember it, because it is going to happen to you. When it happens to you, you will not differ from any other being in the world to whom it has not yet happened. But it is going to happen to every being in the world, but you will be one with those to whom it has already happened.

When it happens, - it may happen to you tonight, - you'll wear the garment for a little while and then in the normal process of time you will take it off. Then at that moment of the discarding of this mold that God used to mold Himself, you will be one with the gods. Your entire inheritance is to inherit the kingdom of heaven. Believe me.

What that garment looks like, I can't describe it. I can describe the sensation, but it doesn't make sense to anyone in the world. But the final act, when he ascends into heaven, and you ascend and live, - I can only describe it as the seraphim. A golden, golden liquid being – and you ascend as a serpent. It doesn't make sense does it?

A human serpent, as described in Isaiah 6:2. The face, the hands, the feet were human but he couldn't describe the glory of the body. It is simply golden liquid light. Because in the resurrection man is above the organization of sex. This garment he used to mold himself and to give man himself.

Blake brought it out in his wonderful poem called "The Gates of Paradise":

> "When weary man enters his cave, he meets
>   his savior in the grave;
> some find a female garment there, and some
>   a male, woven with care,
> Lest the Sexual Garments sweet should grow
>   a devouring winding sheet.
> One Dies! Alas! The Living and the Dead,
>   One is slain, and One is fled."

If this is slain, the mold, it is over. No need for the mold anymore, for he wove among this divided image, male and female, the garment that is immortal, which is above the organization of sex. So he discards then this divided image as far as that individual goes.

He is now clothed in his immortal eternal body and no need for the divided image on which God molded himself and gave Himself to us; that being, being Jesse, which means "I AM". The same name as Jehovah, which is "I AM". The same name as Jesus, which is "I AM".

So I tell you that fantastic mystery of crucifixion. It is true. It begins the play of God. If I went to a play tonight and saw a three hour movie before me on the screen, - I could, as many people do, miscon-strue the role of the actor and make of him, as people do here of a movie actor or stage actor, - make of him an idol, ask him for his signature.

Do all kinds of things that make of him an idol. And then, making of him an idol, he hides from me the message of the play. Here is a play condensed into a few hours that took six thousand years to unfold. And so man's misconception of Jesus Christ has made of Jesus Christ in the eyes of all Christians, an idol; and that idol hides from that man who holds him up as an idol, the true message of God.

God's purpose is to give himself to us without an in-termediary. No intermediary between God and you. Actually he is begetting himself; on you, because He is without origin, the unbegotten.

When he begets himself in you and gives himself to you, completely individualized as you, - and you have no origin, and the reason you have no origin is the child, and you see God's son as your son. Then you will know who you are: the being without father, without mother.

It's a strange thing to say that I a little thing a few years old, - that some fantastic mystery could take place there...and here is this garment which began 58 years ago. And yet on this garment, and the garment which undoubtedly began that preceded it, something was being molded that was unbegotten!

And when it was completely knitted to its perfection, and then I wore the garment that was molded on me, with all the pain that I went through; that I was the being who molded it. And the being who molded it is unbegotten. So the garment I wear, the immortal garment, though begotten, it is being worn now by the unbegotten, God the father. You dwell upon it.

If what I have told you this night seems strange, - if you are here for the first time, or maybe you are here for the hundredth time, it still seems strange, - but it is true. Everything I have told you is true, I have spoken to you from my own spiritual experiences.

We are all on a fabulous pilgrimage moving towards some invisible shrine and God is awakening in us. The world round about us will go on in their journey; and when we are singled out one by one they will laugh at the very thought that he who died a normal death as any other man was that exit, - his final exit; and she by that experience, - do they talk about it, eternalize it?

They smile and continue the journey. Perfectly all right. But I tell you, you too will be called out of the pilgrimage and the voice will speak out of the vast sky: "God walks with them." And someone will question the voice, and the voice will answer, "Yes" and they will turn to you and they will be just as hysterical as they were with me. And the voice in the depths of your own soul will tell you: "God laid himself down within you to sleep, and as he slept he dreamed a dream, he is dreaming that he is you.

And then you will feel the wonderful thrill of being nailed upon this body. But O what a thrill! These whirling vortexes, no pain just joy, ecstatic joy. And then you are on the bed alone and the journey in the soul continues, but they are moving on, but you cannot rest from that moment on.

Everything changes. You see people as you saw them and still they are different. You know their future, you know what they are destined to be; that everyone is destined to have the experience; and to remember in that ecstatic moment where unnumbered ages before he was nailed upon the cross through God's love.

"Unless I die thou canst not live;

But if I die I shall arise again and thou
    with me
And if God dieth not for Man and giveth not
    himself
Eternally for Man, Man could not exist."

And this is the wonderful mystery of life through death. Now here is our story for you this night.

CHAPTER 3

FEED MY SHEEP

This morning's subject is "Feed My Sheep." This is simply saying: practice the truths you have heard, for it means to shepherd the thoughts of the mind. For most of us, our thoughts are like rambling sheep that have no shepherd. We are called upon now to rule the thoughts, to rule the mind.

As you know, the kingdom of Heaven is as a man starting into a far country, and he calls unto himself his servants and gives them his property, his goods. To one he gives five talents, to another he gives two, and to another he gives one "every man according to his several ability", and when he returned he asked for a reckoning.

The one who had five traded and produced another five. He was highly commended and told as he was faithful over a few things he would now be ruler over many. The one who had two, he too traded and produced four, and he too was highly commended and told to enter into the joy of the Lord; but the one who had one was afraid because his master – so he thought – was a hard man, and so he buried his talent in the earth and did not expand it. But I think you know the story.

He was condemned for his misuse of the talent. It was taken from him and given to the one who had the most, the one who had ten. Well, now you have received talents in the last few days or few weeks, each one according to his ability.

Some of us came with more prejudice to overcome, with more superstition, some with other beliefs that did not quite coincide with what we heard from the platform, and many of us had to overcome certain things before we could accept others. So, some got one talent, some two, some five, some maybe more.

Now, a talent that is not exercised, like a muscle that is not exercised, finally sleeps, and as far as we are concerned, it atrophies. It doesn't really die, but it goes so sound asleep, it might just as well not be part of ours. We must practice what we have heard, for without practice the most profound understanding in the world will not produce the desired results.

So a little talent, call it a talent now, if you really expand it, if you exercise it, will be far more profitable than many talents that you do not exercise. Now we will just take one or two of the talents that we offer you – I can't force them upon you we offer you.

Here is a statement from the Book of Amos: "I will sift the House of Israel among all nations, like as corn is sifted in a sieve, yet shall not the least grain fall upon the earth."

I will sift him and scatter him all over the nations of the world, but not the least grain shall fall upon the earth. Do you know who Israel is? Who this Jacob is? Israel means "Is Real."

You can't find it on the earth; don't look for it on the earth and yet you must find him, for I formed him in the womb to be my servant and to bring Jacob, which is Israel, again unto me." [Isaiah 49:5]

So you and I were formed from the womb to be the servant and to bring Jacob unto the Lord. He is scattered all over the world but you will not find him, no not the smallest grain upon the earth, but you will find him within yourself.

For the cue is given in Jacob. Jacob is the smooth skinned lad; he is not like his brother Esau who has hair, which means something external, so the Israel you are looking for this day is the thing you want to realize in the world.

Do not look out and hope to find it or even to be encouraged that you will find it by judging after the appearances of things. Do you seek health for a friend? That's Israel scattered, but not on earth. In all the nations of the world I have scattered the house of Israel, but do not look into the eyes of a doctor for hope.

Do not look into the eyes of the patient for hope of his recovery because you will not find him on earth. Not the least grain has fallen upon the earth. So do you know what you want in this world? If you know exactly what you want, where do you see it?

You see it in the mind of yourself – that's where you see it – so when you know what you want, here is a part of Israel scattered, and you didn't see him on earth, you saw him in the kingdom within you, for the Kingdom of God is within.

So you saw a piece of Israel; now go bring him. I formed you from the womb to be my servant and to bring Jacob again unto me. You take that thing you have seen in the mind's eye, which, to make it practical, we will think of as a friend in need. It may be physical need; maybe he is unwell, or it could be he needs a job.

Well, now, you be the one who will decide what part of Israel you will bring to the Lord and prove to the Lord you are a perfect servant; for the promise is that when you prove you are the perfect servant, then you will no longer be called servant, he will call you his friend.

"I no longer call you servant for now I call you friend for you do whatsoever I command you and, therefore, if you do what I command you, you are no longer my servant, you are my friend."

And now we will commune as a man to a friend, face to face, and after you have had this association for a while, for that is the purpose of it, to move from the servant to the friend, and after we become the friend of God for a while, then we turn to that of the Son. We no longer are the friend, we become his Son, but we cannot recognize the Sonship of God until we first prove ourselves as a servant.

So the servant is to bring Israel. Now, we come back to the friend in need. Represent him to yourself as though he now embodied the state you want him to realize in this world. If it is a job, see him gainfully employed, take your imaginary hand, which is Jacob's hand, and put it into his imaginary hand leave it in that imagined state until it takes on the tones of reality.

When it seems to you real, that you are actually touching him, clothe it with all the reality of the external world. So Jacob clothes himself in the skins of Esau to deceive his father into believing that he, Jacob, was Esau. So you take the Jacob within you, which is the smooth-skinned lad, which is simply now the wish.

You want to congratulate him. You want to hear his voice. You want to hear him tell you he has never been so happy in a job in his life, he has never been so gainfully employed, that he loves going to work, he just loves everything about the job. You actually hear him as though you heard him. Now you clothe it with all the tones of reality.

If you have two talents give it two, if you have five give it five; begin to make it more and more real. The day will come, maybe this day, you will so clothe your Israel with the skins of Esau that you can actually bring it as an objective fact to your Father and prove you are a servant, for he formed you from the womb to actually be his servant; and what is the servant to do – to bring Jacob unto me again.

So here Jacob is scattered – lost in all the minds of men. You won't find him on the earth, you will only find him if you know where to look. Now to prove you know where to look, to prove you are a good servant, go bring me Jacob.

So...when you bring Jacob you bring Jacob clothed in your own mind's eye as though you heard what you want to hear, as though you touched and you witnessed what you would like to touch and see in this world. And when you remain faithful to your vision, the vision will make for itself that perfect body in which to abide.

Then you will see an objective corresponding fact, but it is not there, it is all within your own mind; it is there where he scattered it, it is there where he sustains it. He will simply project it for you onto the screen of space that you may have tangible evidence that you do know how to find and bring Jacob.

If I know how to go searching for my Israel, if I know how to go looking for him and how to clothe him and give him the appearance of reality and I don't do it, then I am not the good servant who took the five talents and expanded them; I am the one who buried it.

Now, some of us are almost afraid to test it because we are comforted if we can believe this without quite putting it to the test, for if we put it to the test and we fail, then we have no faith. We cannot go back to the former comfort that we enjoyed, say, in a more orthodox meeting.

We thought we would find it here, and if I don't test it and prove it to my own satisfaction, then I have neither the old comfort of the orthodox concept nor the comfort that I enjoyed here, for I disproved it. Now I invite you to attempt, if you will, to dis-prove it.

You can't disprove it, but if you go out knowing where to look for your Israel, knowing why you are fashioned from the womb to be a servant, that is the first stage, until you test yourself, until you prove you can do it, you are not a servant, not a servant of the Lord.

But, as you become a servant of the Lord, he will make you his friend. Then the relationship will be on a higher level. You will commune with your Fa-ther as a man does with a friend, face to face. You will not see him as an object in space, but you will actually know how to bring about a wished for state of mind – bring it about at will.

As you can bring about a wished for state of mind, you have made of the deep, which is your Father, a friend, and you will actually know that companionship between the deep of self and you, the being that is really a wonderful imagination. Then the day will come, having been a wonderful friend of God, the seal will be broken and you will be revealed as the Being you really are, which is the Son of God.

Every person in the world is the child of God believing itself to be a man born of man.

I have tried in the past to convince you that your origin is God. It is not what the world would tell you, a little bug, for if you were a little bug, a little spermatozoa, though you seem to embody yourself and expand in the form of a man, your end will be a little spermatozoa, for all ends run true to origins, so whatever the origin, you can determine the end.

I tell you your origin is God, therefore, your end is God. But to arrive at that end, you pass through the stages of the servant, then the friend, then God, which is the Son of God, for I and my Father are one, yet my Father is greater than I. Yes, I do not claim that this union, this oneness, entitles me to the same identical feeling of being Father. I and my Father are one, but my Father is greater than I.

For the thing symbolized that bears witness of this unseen state is not really as great as that which it symbolizes; so we are one and I will know it, and I will see my Father and see that he and I look alike, yet we are Father and Son relationship, but before I can get near it, I must prove I am a good servant.

Now, you take it this morning. We invite you to try it for a friend. We ask you to try it for yourself.

We have given you many angles how to test it, how to think of what you want first and see in your mind's eye, Israel, for when I know clearly in my mind's eye what I want, I am actually looking at Israel, something that is real it is real – but I must clothe it now in what the world calls reality, by giving it external tones; but the thing was real long before it became a visible fact in the world.

I see it in my mind's eye by making as vivid and as life-like a representation as possible of what I would see and what I would do and what I would actually hear were I physically present in such a situation now. When I see it clearly I am looking into the eyes of Israel and I found him scattered in the world but not on the earth, for it is not on earth that I see him. I see him in my mind.

Now I am looking at it, and thinking of it, but the secret is to think from it, to occupy that state and get into it. When I get into it I will clothe it with reality. I can think of a place and then close my eyes and assume that I am in that place. When I assume

I am in the place, I am clothing it with what the world calls reality.

It was real before I clothed it. When I saw it clearly this was Israel – but he wants me to bring him, and the only way I can test that I can bring him and prove that I am the servant is to occupy the state. So, I occupy the feeling of my wish fulfilled.

When I get into the feeling of the wish fulfilled and remain faithful to that state, then I am walking in my vision and, as we are told, if one would only advance confidently in the direction of his dream and endeavor to live the life which he has imagined, he will meet with a success unexpected.

Let me remain faithful to my vision by occupying my vision – don't just see it. He demands that I bring him, and bring Jacob again unto the Lord. So Jacob is not a man who walked the face of the earth thousands of years ago, and Israel is not a nation now gathered together on the shores of Africa – he scatters the house of Israel in all the nations of the world.

You might have been taught to believe that the person who calls himself a Jew in the presence of a nation is scattered Israel. Don't believe it. Everyone in the world is that which actually contains and holds Israel.

As you think of something and desire it to be a reality in your world, you are seeing Israel. Now he wants you to bring him and he wants you to prove that you can bring him and become the perfect servant of the Lord.

Don't be afraid to be the servant; become the perfect servant of God and then become his friend, and then realize you are his Son. Let us go out determined that we will take the requests brought in here this morning; there were a hundred odd that came in, but there are many more.

Maybe you do not know them; you can take them collectively...but you can take an individual friend, a member of your family, and decide this day you are going to bring about some blessing in the individual's life. You have it.

You have the power to bless, for the power to confer reality on your wish for the friend is the power to bless that friend; if your friend is not well and you want the friend to be well, you simply assume that you and he, or you and she, are carrying on a conversation from a premise which you establish now, and the premise is that he or she never felt better in their lives, and you hear it and you witness it.

Take your hand, your imaginary hand, and embrace them; tell them what you feel about them, actually feel it, and then you do nothing outwardly to make it so; for things that you are going to see are not made of things that do appear.

So you do not prescribe anything for them, you do not change their physical diet, you don't offer any recommendation as to what they should do. You simply assume that they are already the embodiment of the state you desire for them, so you don't start prescribing.

Leave that out completely. You simply walk faithful to your image of the friend and you transform that image in your own mind's eye. You do it and see if you can bring him, because if you can't do that and prove it to yourself, you have not yet proven you are a servant; therefore, the friendship is far removed from you.

Everyone must prove that he is first a servant, as we read in the 49th chapter of the Book of Isaiah, "I formed you from the womb to be my servant and to bring Jacob again unto me." Then I am told even though Israel is not altogether gathered I am blessed. The individual who does it, he doesn't have to bring the whole body of Israel.

If he brings Jacob, one individual transformed and proves he can transform him, he is blessed and receives a certain glory long before the body of Israel is collected and brought back. So here you wonder why he is called the King of Israel.

Why is he called the King? People thought it meant a man who looked out upon a small little nation and thought he was king, or they thought he was King, or even in irony when they said it. He isn't that!

The individual who becomes Son is truly King of the whole vast world of Israel, or the ideas floating in the mind of man. For he is their shepherd, he is their King; he can command any idea to clothe itself in form.

That is the king of Israel; that is the one that can make real a state that is only a wish. "Is Real" is the true Israel. Here, long before we become that, lifted up, we must start to discipline the mind to become the perfect servant. There is no better time to start than now.

If you are afraid to try it, then I wouldn't know what to tell you, because in this place you must test it. We do not have a religion where you just come here and sit on Sundays and gather together and form a nice little friendship this way. This is not that kind of a religion at all. This is all to awaken the mind of man and make him a shepherd, make him something that rules.

In fact, the very word translated "feed" in John 21 is translated many times in the Bible as 'shepherd,' as 'rule.' In the 2nd of Matthew one shall come from Bethlehem – he shall have dominion over Israel. Well, that one he shall rule Israel. The word translated "rule" in the 2nd of Matthew is the same word translated in the 21st of John as "feed." So don't take it literally.

It simply means to take this mind of yours and discipline the whole mind by gathering things together and walking faithful to an invisible state, for Jacob is invisible. You thought he was a man who was a smooth skinned lad – that is the way the mystic has of telling you this is a subjective state that you must learn to clothe with objectivity. You walk faithful to the subjective state, and then in time it takes on the tones and the appearance of something external.

The moment you detach your mind from that state – though at the moment of detachment it had some corresponding external witness, it will begin to fade. If you detach your mind from success in the midst of success, success as a reality outside of you fades and vanishes from your world and then whatever you put your mind on, it takes the place of, proving success was not on the outside at all; it was within you.

You clothed it for a moment and gave it the appearance of reality, but the day you are not faithful to the consciousness of being successful, the seeming solid reality of success vanishes from your world, proving itself to be the shadow it always was and the reality, the light of success, was the idea in you with which you were identified.

So if I assume that I am (and I name it) and I remain faithful to it, it comes out and makes itself seemingly real. If I cease to assume it and sustain it, it slowly vanishes from my world, and if it vanishes I might think the reality was there.

I have forgotten how to bring Jacob. I have forgotten how to bring him to the Lord. So here let us remember where Israel is. It's not in the near East. Israel is scattered in all the nations of the world, in your mind, that is where he is.

And now you have a purpose in this world and if you really love the teaching, as the words are "Lovest thou me?", you say you are faithful. Peter do you love me? He doesn't call him Peter by the way, he calls him Simon.

He never calls him Peter in any parts of the Bible; He is referred to as Peter, but whenever he is addressed by the central figure of the gospels, he always calls him Simon, and Simon means to hear, it means to listen.

Well, have you heard, have you really heard, Simon? Yes. Then do you love what you have heard? Lovest thou me, or what I have told you that I am? I am the thing that I teach; so do you love me? Then Feed My Sheep.

Become ruler of this mind of yours and prove you really love the thing you tell me you have heard. If you have heard it, then you are Simon, and if you have really heard it to the point of acceptance, prove you have accepted it by taking the talent received and expand it.

Don't let the shepherd come and when he asks you for the talent, you say you were afraid and you buried it. Let us not be afraid to actually test the truth of the principles we try to explain here.

So, all these are our truths that we have accepted. Now, some got one, some two, some got five. We have done our best to give you all that we could, unfolded from the Bible.

We showed you the Bible as a mystery; that all your members are buried, not in one little book, but in all the books. They are all telling you the story about yourself. How God became you that you may become God.

How God died to become man in the sense of forgetting that he was God, as he awoke as man. Man walking the earth has no knowledge he is God, and the individual who dares to claim that he is, and tells you that you are, is usually condemned by those who appoint themselves as teachers.

That is the blind leading the blind, and they will call you arrogant if you dare to even demonstrate the power of the mind. And they will tell you that's not right – you are taking back from God the thing that belongs to God. You see, they are sound asleep.

They don't realize that God became man for one purpose, that he may have the companionship of sons as Gods. So man must awaken and realize who he really is, and he realizes that by starting first as a servant.

I have given you, I think, a perfect technique to prove that you are a servant. Try it today! If you succeed in the simplest little way of taking an invisible state and making it become a reality, like the job for a friend or even the getting of a hat, or even the finding of the proper apartment, or even the getting of some little thing you try it.

If you lost something, "Nothing is lost in all my holy mountain," sayeth the Lord, for if it isn't lost it is scattered now in Israel. Prove that it isn't lost. What is it that you have lost?

Well, take it in your own mind's eye and then mentally touch it and mentally appropriate it and feel that you have it, that it is yours now, and remain faithful to that assumption and see if the thing returns. If the thing is recovered, you have proved that you have found Israel, a portion of him anyway, and you know how to take him and clothe him in such tones of reality that you can bring him to the Lord, for the Lord is your own wonderful consciousness.

When you say "I AM" that is the Lord. Go tell them I AM hath sent you. So when you walk in the feeling I am so and so, it is not seen as yet, but that is something you are bringing to the Lord, and the more you feel it to be real, the more natural it becomes; then it clothes itself in external facts, but the external fact is not the truth of it.

Truth and fact oppose each other. Truth does not depend upon fact. Truth depends upon the intensity of your imagination. Therefore, if I actually am intense about it, that is true.

I might tomorrow find a corresponding fact to bear witness − but, as I said earlier, let me not continue in that assumption and the fact will fade, proving it was not reality at all. Reality was in my assumption, and so truth depends not upon fact, but upon the intensity of imagination.

Then you will understand the drama when truth faces what is called fact or reason, and when asked what is the Truth, Truth remains silent. He would not answer because fact or reason thinks that a true judgment must conform to the external reality to which it relates.

If I say, "Aren't these lovely" and I mention something that no one present can see, you say my judgment isn't true, for if it isn't on something on the outside, then what I say has no reality.

I must be suffering from some illusion. If I persist in it, and you cannot see it, then it is hallucination. However, I know from experience that I can take an illusion, and through the medium of an illusion I can relate myself to reality or "Is Real" by walking faithful to what you call my illusion.

I simply assume a state knowing I have found it; it is scattered in the nations of the world and finding it in myself as a desirable state, I appropriate it. Walking faithful to my appropriated state I gradually become it. Disentangling myself from that state eventually, I cease to be it, for that which requires a state of consciousness to embody itself cannot be embodied without such a state of consciousness.

When I know that the whole thing depends upon my appropriation of the parts of Israel to bring Jacob to my Father, then I will start to do it, and then my talents will run from five to ten and to twenty, and finally when I have all these talents I will be worthy of being a friend.

When I have been faithful in a few things, he will make me Lord over much. Then he will tell me I no longer call you servant, I call you friend, for you did what I commanded you.

Now, having done what I commanded you, you are my friend indeed. We will walk in that association for a while, communing with the deep, knowing the deep of self is my real being that men call God. I won't see him as another.

I will commune with him as though he were another, and he and I will talk across that invisible state just as though man spoke face to face with a friend, for after this invisible state when I commune with the deep is reached to a point of complete satisfaction, the last seal will be broken.

He will break the seal and reveal me as his son, and when I see him and look into his face he will be just like me and I will be like him. Then you will know the mystery of the Epistle of John - "Beloved what manner of love" just imagine what love God has bestowed upon us that we should be called the Sons of God.

And then, although at this moment, this very moment, that I feel it from the deep, I don't quite know what I am like or what he is like; yet I do know this much, that when I see Him I will know Him. And why will I know Him? Because I'll be like Him.

I will look right into the mirror of my own being and realize it was for that purpose that I the Father embodied myself as man, hoping that eventually he would awaken and become a conscious being, moving completely from a passive reflector to a conscious cooperator in my Kingdom. So, man gradually moves from the passive state to the active state, and the process is the servant, the friend, the Son.

CHAPTER 4

THE FOURFOLD GOSPEL

As you know, and I think you do, the Bible is a mystery. A mystery to be known only by revelation. As I told you in the past, a mystery is not a matter to be kept secret but a truth which is mysterious in character. The four Gospels are the flower of the entire Bible.

Everything that was promised Israel, as we have it recorded in the 39 books of the Old Testament, came into flower – in the fulfillment of the four Gospels. But even to this day, 2000 years later, many women came seeking, - in the Bible, - for the Christ of whom the prophets spoke and whose coming is told. As we are told, the prophets who prophesied of the grace that was to be yours inquired and searched about that salvation.

They inquired what person or time was indicated by the Spirit of Christ within them when predicting the sufferings of Christ and the subsequent glory, but they could not find him. They are all looking for a man, and today the whole vast Christian world turns to a man. Those who deny it think in terms of a man that they deny, but they do not know the Christian mystery.

Paul makes the statement: "From now on we will regard no one from the human point of view, even though we once regarded Christ from a human point of view we regard him thus no longer." Yes, even though I once thought of Christ from a human point of view I think of him so no longer. It is something entirely different. To understand this mystery we have to find the root, and that is in the Old Testament.

What did they promise? They found it in the Messianic Book Isaiah 11:1-3; one of the many chapters, but this one is prominent. "There shall come forth a stem from the stump of Jesse and a Branch will go out of that root, and the Spirit of the Lord shall be upon him. The imagery turns from a root – from a Branch, from a stem, into a man.

"And the Spirit of the Lord shall rest upon him; the Spirit of understanding, the Spirit of Knowledge, the Spirit of Counsel, the Spirit of the fear of the Lord." All these will be upon him.

"And he shall not judge by what his eyes see, or desire by what his ears hear." So here, something is said about a Branch, something is said about a stump out of which the Branch will come.

We search the Scripture and we find in the Book of Daniel: "And the king said: 'I beheld in the visions of my head as I lay in bed, and behold, a watcher, a holy one, came down from heaven. He cried aloud and said this,' 'Hew the tree down, cut off its branches, strip off its leaves and scatter its fruit. But leave the stump.'"

Do not disturb the stump. And now he turns from the imagery of the tree with its branches, leaves and stump, to that of a man. "Let him be watered with the dew of heaven," speaking now of the stump, - and it becomes now a man.

"Let him dwell with the beasts of the field. Take from him the mind of a man and give to him the mind of a beast. And let seven times pass over him until he knows that the Kingdom of Heaven, or the Most High rules the kingdom of men, and gives it to whom he will."

And you ask: "What is it all about?" This is the prophecy that is fulfilled in our Gospel. The word

Jesse means "I AM". It is called "The stump of Jesse." The word "I AM" which we call Jehovah, the name of God. In its root meaning means "to fall" or "To cause to fall." The only Being that fell – this tree of life – is God Himself, and for us God fell. He sacrificed Himself to redeem us, to give us life in ourselves.

The mystery of life through death, - the death of God, - is that stump. So I am this branch. Now we turn and study the word "Branch". The stump is "I AM". The Branch comes out of the stump of Jesse. The first presentation is in Matthew.

Matthew presents the Lord as a king. So where is the Branch identified in the Bible as a king? You find it in Jeremiah 23:5: "Behold, the days are coming, says the Lord, when I will raise up for David a righteous Branch, and he shall reign as king."

So here we find the presentation of this Branch, which is not a tree, - we see now it is a man. Here he is presented as a king. So Matthew gives him the genealogy of a king. He comes down through the royal line.

Matthew begins the book: "This is the book of the genealogy of Jesus Christ, the son of David." David is the source of the dynasty. The first king of Israel was Saul, chosen by the people, but Jehovah rejected

Saul and chose David, and David is the first king of Israel, as chosen by God.

This is the book of the genealogy of Jesus Christ, son of David. When I trace the genealogy of a king I must always begin at the source of the dynasty and come down and finish with the king. When I trace the genealogy of a man, I begin with his father and go back as far as I may; but not with a king.

You do not say: "This is king so and so, the son of so and so." You go right back to the source of the dynasty then you bring it forward and it culminates in the king himself.

That is how we get the genealogy of a king. That is what Matthew does in presenting the Lord as king to fulfill Jeremiah 23:5. Mark presents him as a servant, therefore there is no need for a genealogy. The perfect, the ideal servant. So God is now presented as a servant. And here, - where is the branch of the servant? Zech. 3:8.

"Behold I will bring forth my servant, the Branch. All this is prophecy, it hasn't brought him forth, he is bringing him forth. So, Mark does not have a genealogy. Who are you? "I am the servant of the Lord." Well, that's good enough.

If you are the servant of the Lord there is no need for any further credentials. So his credentials are simply his position in life as the ideal servant, - that's Mark. In Mark 10:5 he makes this statement: "I come not to be served but to serve." He is the servant.

Luke presents him as the ideal man, - Jehovah's man. Where is the Branch concerning it? Read Zech. 6:12. First of all Isaiah claims it in the 40th Chapter: "Behold the man". He doesn't use the word Branch, but Zechariah to fulfill the prophecy brings in the Branch:

"Behold, the man whose name is the Branch." So, Luke presents him the ideal man and should have a genealogy. When you read the two genealogies in Matthew and Luke they differ.

At the beginning of David, the king, they part, and David's older son, Nathan becomes the line through which Luke takes Jesus Christ. His younger son Solomon becomes the one he takes bringing him into a king. Here you find a complete different genealogy for fourteen generations and another fourteen following them.

Here you have these many generations where they are entirely different background and people think you can't be telling the story of the same person, but people don't know the mystery. You are presenting not a person, you are presenting, not a man, you are presenting something altogether different.

Christ is not a man, a king, a servant. Christ that saying, is a series of mystical experiences through which God reveals Himself for the salvation of man, - that is Christ. The whole vast New Testament is based upon the assumption that a certain series of events happened in which God revealed Himself in action for the salvation of man. Did they happen?

We are told in the Scripture they did happen. I claim the evangelists were telling their own story, as told us in the end of Luke: "And they told what had happened." Moffitt takes that phrase and describes it and translates it; 'They related their own experience." They are relating a series of mystical happenings in the soul of the individual where God revealed Himself in these actions for the salvation of that individual.

So, Luke presents God as the ideal man: "Behold, the man whose name is the Branch." He must have a genealogy and this goes all the way back unbroken to Adam, the son of God. John, on the other hand, presents him as God Himself – no need of a genealogy. Now, this you find is Isaiah 4:2. "And the day is coming," it's always in the future, it's all prophecy - "When the Branch of Jehovah will be beautiful and glorious."

And men are still looking for this Branch to flower in some mighty conqueror who will come and save humanity from the tyrants who are loose in the world. He doesn't come that way. They denied he was a king because they did not read carefully. "My kingdom is not of this world."

They are still expecting him in some way to entrench himself in the world and establish a kingdom; and reveal what they believe to be David's kingdom, - and all these must be spiritualized. All the characters mentioned as his background, his genealogy, are states of consciousness.

Here it begins: "This is the book of the genealogy of Jesus Christ, the son of David." The very end of the genealogy Joseph's father is called Jacob. Matthew 1:17 and two verses on the 20th verse: "The angel of the Lord appears unto Joseph in a dream and says: "Joseph, son of David, do not fear to take Mary your wife."

Three verses before it is said in the genealogy that his father was Jacob, and just a few verses down the angel of the Lord addresses him as "Joseph, son of David." Here in the genealogy Joseph is called the father, and the genealogy begins with "Jesus Christ, son of David."

Don't you see it? You have to spiritualize all of these characters. They are states of consciousness. They are not persons any more than Jesus Christ is a person. Jesus Christ is that series of events unfolding like a tree in man for the salvation of that man in whom this series unfolds. But man cannot think that way if he wants to personify it and put it in a wall, or in some little hole and do something with it. And it isn't that.

So, here in Mathew we find the presentation of God as a king. In Mark he is presented as the ideal servant. In Luke God is presented as the ideal man and in John – God Himself. So in John he speaks and calls Himself constantly "I AM". "I am the vine; I am the way; I am the truth; I am the resurrection; I am the door." All through he is emphasizing who He really is, the Being that you are.

But the series of events, I promise you, will unfold within you. When they unfold within you, you know who you are, and you could no more keep it to yourself than the evangelist who experienced Christ could have kept it to himself. They couldn't. Having experienced Christ, they could not keep their experience of Christ to themselves, so they told it.

Now let us show you what Luke tells us in his own words. Why they translated it this way I do not know. Luke begins his book: "Inasmuch as many have undertaken to encircle a narrative of the thing which have been accomplished among us, as it was revealed to us by those who were eye witnesses from the beginning, it seemed good to me also, having observed closely for sometime past."

Now that phrase, "For sometime past", is a translation of the Greek word Zecharias, which means "from above". When it is used in the 3rd chapter of John it is used "From above", when he said to Nicodemus: "You must be born from above. Except you be born from above you cannot enter the Kingdom of Heaven." Yet here in the book of Luke the same words, no alteration, the identical word is translated in this phase: "For sometime past."

So he is telling you if you go back to the original tongue where he got it. "Having observed all things closely from above it seems good to me also to write an orderly account to you Theophilus, - a lover of God, one who seeks God, - and he is telling him where he got it. He is not making any claims that his arrangement is a greater chronological arrangement of the false material.

What he is telling us is he got it from above and he is going to write it in an orderly arrangement which he claims is a better arrangement, better understood by man. So he begins with a birth and he ends, for man's sake, with a crucifixion. That is not the way in which Luke got it, for Luke is not his name. All this is anonymous.

Whoever calls himself Luke did not receive it in that order. But he thinks it is a better arrangement to be understood by mortal mind, until they themselves have the experience. So, what the Gospels are telling us, believe it. Believe it for the works' sake.

Now he tells us how to prove the Law of God and in proving the Law of God you may believe his Promise. Then he tells us what to do about the Law of God: "Ask anything in my name" – don't forget the name, - the name is "I AM", - "And it will be done unto you."

Don't call it by any other name, and when you call upon my name, call with my name. Don't say: "In the name of 'I AM'" Just declare yourself to be "I AM". I am what? You name it. Whatever you want to be just name it, but call with my name.

So, call "I am healthy, I am lovely, I am loved, I am anything you think lovely in your world, call upon it by calling with the name. Then he tells them: "I come to testify of things that I know and that I have seen. If you will not receive the testimony that I bring from things of earth, how will you receive the testimony of mine if I tell you of things of Heaven."

Let me give you a vision of mine that happened many years ago to show you how it was revealed to me long before it began to awaken in me. Just like the vision of the 4th of Daniel, only in my case it wasn't a tree. But just as he starts off the vision: "The visions of my head as I lay in bed." Suddenly I saw this fabulous field, and consciousness followed vision and I entered the field. It had no limit, it was infinite.

At first I thought them to be flowers, long tall flowers like sunflowers. As I approached them they were not flowers, they were all rooted like a flower into the earth; but they were human faces, everyone was a face. As I came upon them they moved in concert as though someone led them in some orchestra, and they all moved and bent over. If one smiled they all smiled. They all did everything in concert.

While I walked among them admiring these beautiful human faces, that were anchored like a flower, I realized right at that moment that I, - not comparable to them in beauty, - nothing in that rhythm and yet I enjoyed greater freedom, limited as I was, than all of them put together. They moved in concert and I had freedom of movement even though my motion was not in harmony.

I had freedom of choice even if I made the wrong choice. I could choose evil, they could do nothing.

They could do nothing of themselves. And I realized that with all of my limitations, I was greater. I could make a mistake and they couldn't. I could actually move without the consent of another; they couldn't.

And beautiful as they were, I realized how much infinitely greater I was, limited as I was, because I was detached from that field. And I thought in the depths of me that at one time I must have been one of that orchestra. And God in his infinite mercy, fell with me, and then took up residence in me. Then seven times had to pass over me, the fiery ordeal.

I had to be given a human face, - "Take the mind of man from him and give him the mind of a beast." Let him know this was the beast of the field. "Sever everything from him; cut off the branches, strip the leaves, scatter the fruit but don't disturb the roots," – and the root is God Himself. That is Jesse. But, "Seven times must pass over him until he knows that the Most High rules the kingdom of men and gives it to whom He will."

And He gives it in that moment that He gives us Christ; and Christ is that series of mystical experiences taking place in the individual soul, for the soul's salvation. I can see that field of flowers now, perfectly beautiful human faces, - not a blemish, everything perfect, everything in perfect rhythm as if some invisible director directed them.

You and I were once part of that harmony and then the harmony became broken for our salvation, and we descended because God descended with us. He didn't push us out. The word He Vau He means "to fall" and that is the root of the verb Yod He Vau He, which we call Jehovah, the great sacred name. The name by which all things are made. So, Matthew, Mark, Luke and John presents this mystery of the Branch. I tell you it grows in us.

As Blake said: "The Gods of the Earth and the Sea sought through Nature to find this Tree, but their search was all in vain, there grows one in the human brain." And that tree is turned down.

If you saw the human being and take off the skin and see just the nervous system, it is just like an inverted tree. Where the brain is, is the root, and the whole tree grows down. But that tree is going to be turned up, and one day you will see it turned up and there will be a complete severance of your being, called the "Curtain of the temple", - and then you, that was living down not even knowing it, will be turned right up and all the currents of eternity are now reversed in you, and from then you grow up.

The vision I had of this many years ago startled people. I first told it in San Francisco. Why the reaction was horrible. Yet the Book of Mark, speaking of the servant of the Lord, who is the Branch, speaks of it.

When the Lord opened the eyes of the blind man and said: "What do you see?" He said: "I see men like trees walking."

There it is: "I see men like trees walking." That night I had this vision of the majesty of man when he is turned up. You will think, "How can I be a tree?" The beauty, the joy when you see it, - something altogether different; but how can you describe it?

You can't describe it to the satisfaction of anyone because who wants to be a tree? And yet, here inverted, - and we are called the Branch. Don't forget it. "And there shall come forth from a stem from the stump of Jesse," from the stump of "I AM", "and a branch will grow out of his roots.

And the Spirit of the Lord shall rest upon him, the spirit of wisdom and understanding, the spirit of counsel and might, the spirit of knowledge and the fear of the Lord. (Isaiah 11:1-3)

"Fear" means "the reverence of the Lord." Again these same four, Matthew, Mark, Luke and John is revealed to us in a strange way when the child is given a name. Isaiah 9:6. "For to us a child is born, to us a son is given; and the government will be upon his shoulder, and his name will be called Wonderful Counselor."

Two entirely different experiences; a child is born, a son is given. Don't put a comma between Wonderful and Counselor as so many Bibles have. Bear in mind there were no punctuation marks in the ancient Hebrew, not even breaks or paragraphs, it is all continuous.

There are four names given in keeping with the fourfold Gospel. "His name shall be called; Wonderful Counselor, Mighty God, Everlasting Father, Prince of Peace." There are four titles. Wonderful Counselor, - that is Omniscience itself. You can add nothing to a Being who is completely awake; they would not have the automatic answer. So, here is Omniscience. Mighty God, - Divine Omnipotence.

That is when the third title comes. Then, Prince of Peace, that is at the very end when you are about to take off the garment for the very last time, as told us in the book of John. "My peace I leave with you, not as the world giveth, give I unto you." He gives us peace that is beyond understanding.

You can't disturb that peace, for he is the "Prince of Peace." He is an "Everlasting Father", - he is Father forever. "When you see me you see the Father." "Almighty God." – A might beyond the wildest dreams of anything you have ever seen. And when you see that Might you see it personified as a man. You look into his eyes and you see might as you have never known it before – and it is a man. Then "Wonderful Counselor".

He promises he will send the Counselor. When he withdraws he will send the servants who have the understanding to follow him as he reveals what happened to him. So when you read the Gospels, whether it be Matthew, Mark, Luke or John, do not see a man walking through the pages, see the magnificence of Christ the Branch unfolding in you, and it takes root.

There will come out a root from that stump. How does it take root? Well, you first hear the story and you believe it. Then the Word is planted. When one believes it, he has accepted the Word. The Word as translated in the Book of John is called Logos.

"In the beginning was the Word," that is the Greek Logos: "And the Word was with God and the Word was God." That is really the translation of the Hebrew which means "The word of God, which contains within itself the power of it's own expression."

That "Word" in the first verse of the Book of John is Christ. "In the beginning was the Word and the Word was with God and the Word was God." Now turn to Isaiah 55:11. "So shall my word be that goes forth from my mouth; it shall not return to me empty, but it shall accomplish that which I purposed and fulfill that where I sent it."

So the word when it comes is The Word called Christ. I tell you the story, believe it. The minute you believe it you have accepted it, it has fallen on fertile ground. It will then take root; and the word contains within itself the power of it's own expression. The whole vast program of God for man's salvation is contained in that Word, "the seed", and it falls upon man and man hears it. He either believes it or he rejects it.

Here we move across the world and seven times pass over us until one day we hear it with acceptance and then the little root takes place in that stump of Jesse, the stump of "I AM." Then out of it comes the Branch, and then the Spirit of the Lord descends upon him. From then on he moves and you can't stop him. You can't earn it, - accept it.

Believe the story as it was intended when you first listened; completely misunderstood through the centuries. He tells it of a certain individual who was born in a strange way; raised in a strange way and died a horrible death.

That's not the story at all. If I would comfort you with the death it is Romans 6:5: Here we are told: "If we have been united with Christ in a death like his, we shall be united with him in a resurrection like his." He uses the past tense when it comes to death, the future when it comes to resurrection.

So the unity took place in his death, or He fell, and all of us are in it and now he is asking us for acceptance of the Word. We have union with him in a death like His, we shall have union with him in a resurrection like His. And He resurrects us one after the other by a series of fantastic, wonderful mythical experiences one after the other.

We can't contrive them, they come like a thief in the night when least expected. Everything said in the Gospel concerning the central figure is all about you, from beginning to end. I tell you the death has already taken place, even though the death took place to free us all. It has been felled.

You downed the tree, cut off the branches, that is all over. Stripped the leaves, scattered the fruit, given the mind of a beast. Well, haven't we the mind of a beast? Go back 20 years. What beast in the world would have conceived by ovens to burn innocent people by the millions? Isn't that the mind of a beast?

Have you read here recently the current stories of Stalin, the things the man did with those even in the most intimate circles? That no one felt at ease in his presence? From Molotov down, all like little children shaking, everyone of them. It came out last Sunday in the Times, in yesterday's Observer, in today's New York Times.

All these stories because today is the tenth anniversary of his death. There is no beast that would have done the things the man did to his own people. He hated everything in the world and so did Hitler. So, "Take the man's mind from him and give him the mind of a beast."

Who gave the order? God. And this is the order from on high. Now in the eyes of the world they seemed to be so far advanced because they were so powerful. In the exercise and misuse of power they are on the down, they are descended. Seven times must pass over the mind of the beast before they could accept the story of Christianity.

Both rejected it, both called it foolish, said the whole thing was stupid, the opium of humanity, said one, quoting his master, Karl Marx. The other looked upon Christianity as the weakest thing in the world. The Christ to him was nothing but a weakling because he couldn't kill. He said "Put up the sword" and "Turn the other cheek" and "Father forgive them they know not what they do."

So here you see the beast of beasts and all at God's command. "Take from him the mind of a man and give him the mind of a beast, and let his lot be among the beasts, but do not disturb the root, leave the stump and let it be watered with the dew of Heaven." And then there is a reversal and all of a sudden the stump puts out a shoot.

It can't put out the shoot until it first heard the Word of God. We must all go and tell the world and it must start in Jerusalem and spread to Judea, to Sumer, to the ends of the earth. Go and tell it. And some will accept it and some will reject it. Those that reject it, alright, because seven times must pass over. And what are the seven times?

Read the 3rd chapter of the Book of Daniel. "And heat the furnaces seven times more than they were wont to be." Then comes the three Hebrew boys and they are put into the furnace, clothed. Then the king said: "Were there not three?" They answered "Yes". "But I see four and the fourth has the form of the Son of God." Three were put in, the three-fold man, the three dimensional man, but goes with them the fourth, God Himself.

For the fourth is God Himself. When they came out, "Their hair was not singed, nor even the smell of fire upon their garments." Then he, Nebuchadnezzar, worshiped the God of Israel, worshiped the

God of Shadrach, Meshach and Abednego. The whole thing is a mystery to be unfolded in the simple way it began by telling you of Christ of the Scripture. He is unfolding in you in a series of events, revealing to you your salvation.

Peter in his Epistle said: "The prophets told how they searched and inquired about the grace that was to be yours: and how they inquired about their salvation, asking what person, what time was indicated by the Spirit of Christ within him when prophesying and predicting of the sufferings of Christ and the subsequent glory." But they didn't find it. They couldn't find the Christ of whom they wrote and whose coming they foretold, because they were looking for a man.

Today they are still looking for a man, and looking for a time. They think maybe 1963 will bring it, or 1964. All through the ages people have thought a certain moment in time was the coming of Christ, or the coming of a person; but he doesn't come that way. He comes in you and when you have him, you share him with everyone who will listen.

Many will say, because they know you so well: "Don't I know him? Isn't he Mary's child? Isn't his father named George? Doesn't he work in the factory with me. I know him so what is he talking about?"

They expect an entirely different kind of person to come. They don't expect the garment to have in it an experience that no mortal man could possibly have. It all happens in the depths of the soul of a man. Then he goes back and he sees where it was all foretold but: "Naught could he himself foresee."

It's all there but he couldn't dig it out anymore than the scholars can until it happens. And after it comes to the surface in him he is bewildered. When the dust settles so that he really can talk about it without excitement, a few will listen and the majority will turn their backs. They say: "He's talking about a Christ I never heard of before.

I'd rather have my old Christ, because to him I can kneel, to him I can say a prayer in the hope that he will have compassion on me and respond; but this Christ." A series of mystical experiences in the soul of man where the whole tree has fallen, and suddenly the tree that was felled and downed turns around?

And then the whole thing goes back into the stump itself, the skull of man, and from then on it begins to really grow; and then he knows what the glory is Paul spoke of?"

"For there is laid up for me in Heaven a crown of glory." He himself grows it, no one puts it upon him.

It is a living crown, not a crown as the human eye sees when they see the queens crown. Do you know of any crown comparable to the antlers of a stag? Did you ever see such majesty in your life when you see this beautiful thing. Did you ever see such majesty as a tree in full bloom? No.

Don't even try to visualize it, because it frightens people. The writer of the Book of Mark could see it correctly. What do you see now with the eye open: "I see men like trees walking." Believe the story as I told you this night concerning Matthew, Mark, Luke and John. You are the fourfold man. One presents you with a king to fulfill the 23rd Chapter of Jeremiah. He said: "I have come to fulfill the Scripture. Scripture must be fulfilled in me.

"And beginning with Moses and all the prophets he interprets with them in all the Scriptures the things concerning Himself." It was all about this being that you are. Then comes the presentation of the ideal servant.

Zech. 3:8: "Behold, I will bring my servant the Branch." Behold, the man whose name is the Branch. Then comes the fulfillment of the 4th of Isaiah. All must be fulfilled. So, these four branches must take root and all grow and mature in man. We have king, servant, the ideal man, and God Himself.

CHAPTER 5

RELEASE BARABBAS &
CRUCIFY JESUS!

Some among us feel that life should be a perpetual increase of the things you love. That, to me, is the art of living.

In man's ability to live in the end, to live in the feeling of the wish fulfilled, lies man's capacity to live the more abundant life. I do not care what your objective is; feeling that you have it is living a more, abundant life. First, let us turn to three who were awake, and by three I mean three men.

The whole purpose of life is to awaken and join the chorus of awakened humanity, which is God. We will turn to a great poet, one who passed from this sphere only within the last two or three years, Walter de La Mare.

"So flows experience, the vast without. It is the microcosm of the soul within, The day-distracted eye may doubt, But no longer as the dreams begin." Think of it! This vast "without" is the microcosm of the soul within. The day-distracted eye cannot believe it, but you take this and expand it to the nth degree and see that the "vast without" is only the microcosm of the soul within. How can man believe it?

Now we will turn to the great bard – Shakespeare: Everything in the world is the projection of something that activated within myself. I meet a friend and I say that I love him and I see in him something that I would like to change.

Everything in this world is the microcosm of this vastness in my own being. Everything in the world, "no matter what it is, all the so-called evil could be changed, would man, observing, distill it out." If I knew this I could look at anything, any condition, as a scientist could look at bubbling mash, and know I could extract something from it that is good.

Blake tells us: "He who does not imagine in stronger and broader lineaments, and in stronger and brighter light than his perishing and mortal eye can see, does not imagine at all." This is in a way a parable. A parable is a story told to illustrate a truth.

In Second Corinthians 3:6, in the letter which Paul writes to the Corinthians – these are not the people of Corinth. You are Corinthians, for these are stories of the mysteries, and so this is Corinth, so the letters are addressed to those who are interested in rising to another level of consciousness: "We are the ministers of a new covenant, not written in the code but in the spirit."

Now remember the teaching: "The letter killeth but the spirit giveth life." So we are ministers of a new covenant. You be the judge, for I am not here to judge you. But if I came and whispered in your ear that you were harboring a robber, would you react violently? You be the judge, but I will tell you a story, in the code written in the form of a letter. This is the story of Jesus and Barabbas.

Now it was the season of the year when it was customary to release a man who was imprisoned. "Whom will you have me release unto you? Barabbas or Jesus? And they cried, Release Barabbas! Crucify Jesus!" "And when the wife of Pilate said to him, will you do this thing? he washed his hands," etc.

Now you take that, and that is the code – but what does it really mean? That it took place, actually? We are warned of those who "depart from the truth," and those who think that the resurrection has already taken place, they have wandered from the truth, for if it has already taken place then I cannot know the power that resurrects every dream in the world.

The resurrection must be taking every moment in time in all men. The Passover does not take place at a certain time of year, like Easter. The Passover takes place every moment of the day, if we are willing to pass over into another state.

There must always be a passing over from one state to a higher state. So, which will you have me release, the robber or Jesus? Which will you let go of, and to which will you hold fast? I must release the robber, for I am housing him. Who is he?

If this moment you want something and reason tells you that you cannot have it, than you are entertaining the thief that robs you of being what you want to be in this world. This is the "son of Satan," something in me that robs me of that other Son who will save me. The thing that will save me from what I am, is Christ Jesus. And what is keeping you from what you want? That is Barabbas.

So, they crucify Jesus; they fix the state desired. The whole drama takes place in you. You must release

Barabbas and crucify the Lord. You must learn the art of doing it. I can tell it best now by telling a case history I have just received.

This is what she told me: She had a neighbor, a woman who had been divorced for nineteen years, and who was up to her ears in debt. She worked hard but she could not get beyond a day-to-day existence. She could not afford a vacation, though she had one due.

In four weeks college was starting and her son wanted to go to college, and there was no means with which to send him. She had prayed over her problem, but she had got nowhere, and then she asked this lady who wrote the letter to pray for her.

This lady explained to her this teaching that I am giving you here, and then she did what follows for her neighbor. She asked her first: what do you really want? Well, this woman had been divorced for nineteen years and she had lost her faith in men, but still she said that above all else she would like to be happily married and out of debt.

Every night for a month this lady from the class here went to her neighbor's house and talked with her and made her think of the qualities she most wanted in a husband: gentleness, kindness, tolerance, attentiveness, honesty, etc. All the qualities she felt a man should have she had to name over and over. And then the lady asked her: "Can you feel the embrace of such a man?" and the other lady said: "Yes, I think I can."

And then she did something else. She went through the marriage ceremony with her neighbor, the part of putting on the ring and hearing the words pronouncing the couple man and wife. And then she left her neighbor with the suggestion that she sleep in that state and promised her that she would do the same thing – that is, sleep in the state herself of having just seen her neighbor married.

They did this for four weeks. And then a man came into her office (the office of the neighbor) and in talking, he asked her where she was going for her vacation. She was ashamed to confess that she was not going anywhere, so she said she thought maybe she might go up to the High Sierras, and the man said: "Then you must be my guest, for I own a hotel up there." He booked rooms for three of them: the woman and her son, and the lady who had helped her. The man was very kind and helpful to them.

He told the woman that he had lost his wife a few months before. But he also told her that he would never marry again. The woman had grown fond of him and was distressed by this and told the lady who had helped her. "What will I do now? He is never going to remarry. He said so."

The lady said, "You are happily married, so we are not going to discuss this. You slept every night in the feeling of having a wonderful husband, a man who has the qualities you desire. So how can we discuss the matter? You are married."

That was over two years ago. She has been married to this man for two years. Yes, he changed his mind about marrying again. He is sending this woman's son through college.

She said recently to the lady who had helped her with this teaching: "You have no idea how kind and good he is, how wonderful." The woman said: "Haven't I?" She said: "I set up these qualities with you and helped you. Do you think I don't know what he is like?"

Now back to the crucifixion. You must release the consciousness Barabbas, the robber. This woman robbed herself for nineteen years. She robbed herself of the lovely things of life. Finally she faced a choice: either Barabbas released or Jesus released, or Jesus crucified.

If I want to be anything in this world and say I cannot be that, then I am robbing myself of the ability to be it. Man can be anything in this world that he wants to be, for man awake is the son of God. There is only one son and that is Christ Jesus and that son is human imagination, the only Christ Jesus in the world. There will never be another.

So I look out on the world and I think it towers over me and I do not know that actually it is the microcosm of the soul within me. If I do not know it, start the dream to prove it. Can you feel embracing arms around you? This woman began the dream and then realized it.

The whole vast world without only mirrors the soul within. The Passover means the passing over into another. When we were children we were told that Jesus sacrificed himself for us 2,000 years ago. That is belief in a lie. You depart from the truth if you believe the crucifixion is already past.

It is not over; it is constant fact every moment of time. It is not past and it must be continually taking place. The whole vast drama unfolds within us. We can distill out of any situation the good that is in it. You can take it as you take a mash and distill the essence from it.

You are told the Old Testament is one covenant and the New Testament is another covenant. Do not believe it. There is only one Book. When you find the spirit of it that sets you free, that is the new covenant. The letter killeth, the spirit giveth life.

Take the same "code" and re-read it, and strike as it were the rock and then draw forth the water and make it into wine. Rock, as we are told you, means literal fact. Water means psychological understanding; wine means the application of that truth. If you know this, every dream in the world can be realized.

In the capacity to live in the wish fulfilled lies your capacity for living the more abundant life. These stories which I tell you are "stone" if you take them literally, but "water" if you understand them, and then they become "wine" if you apply what you have learned. You can get all the results as this lady got them.

But the lady who is now married, though she is happy she may slip into a way of life and forget how this was brought about. People quickly "recover" from this teaching. I could tell you many stories of friends of mine who wanted help and who told me the dream they wanted to come true. And with them I listened as though I heard and looked as if I saw what they wanted to see, and the thing became true in their world.

There is the story of my brother-in-law, told in one of my books. He knows that story is there, and though all my other books are in evidence in his library, that particular one he has put up so high that no one can reach it. He is such a factual, realistic person that though the dream he wanted most in the world was brought about, now he is embarrassed when he thinks about the way it was brought about. He is too down-to-earth to want to remember it. So I tell you we must remember the story of the crucifixion.

As Paul said: "I die daily." I should be dissatisfied: I should have always a "divine dissatisfaction" and transcend and transcend, to become one of the awakened brothers. I cannot live on what I learned today.

Extend the borders of your tent. Not only must I grow, but also I must also outgrow or I am not growing. Let no one tell you that this world is your end. You are a fabulous being. You do not change worlds by spatial travel; you change by a change in consciousness. Subjective or objective is determined by the level on which my consciousness is focused.

I ask you to construct a little drama that implies you have realized your dream. This lady went through the ceremony of marriage and with a man who had all the qualities she wanted. And in five weeks the drama began to unfold. The whole thing took three months and now this lady is happily married.

Everything you want is within, for the vast without is only the microcosm of the soul within. But though you doubt, you will no longer doubt when the dream begins. "He who does not imagine in stronger and brighter lineaments than this perishing and mortal eye can see, does not imagine at all."

Smell a rose. See it. You can see and smell it the degree your attention is centered on it. If you let it posses your mind you will see it and smell it. That is being creative. You see what you want to see, and enter into and live it as if it were true. Others may call it fantasy and when it becomes real they will believe you did it this way. But let anyone else believe what they want to believe.

I told a friend of mine who was critical without taking the trouble to know what he was being critical of: your taste and your opinion do not qualify you to criticize. You must first know what I am trying to do, and then you may venture your opinion. But if you do not know what I am doing or what I am trying to do, then how can presume to criticize?

Everything in this world is done through imagination, but many people do not see it. But do you know of anything that was made that not first imagined? But you make your dream and walk in it as if it is true, and others will come along like workmen following you to execute it.

Edison told Tesla that it would not be possible to have alternating current. Edison said it could not be, but Tesla told him: "I can see it. I can see the machine. And I am starting it and stopping it, and I am taking out the kinks in it before I make it in the laboratory."

Read about the life of Nikola Tesla. They called him mad before he died. You know why? He said he was communicating with Edison, who was dead. Because others could not understand this, they called Tesla mad. Ecclesiastes 3 states: "I am the beginning and the end" and "there is nothing to come that has not been and is."

Creation is finished. We are only becoming aware of increasing portions of that which is. If everything is, am I still creative? I am in this sense: I become a selector of that aspect of reality to which I want to respond and then I bring that into my world. It is like taking the alphabet. Shakespeare and Blake used only twenty-six letters.

A moron would use exactly twenty-six letters. But think of the difference. Think of an infinite alphabet and we select what we will from that alphabet. But you just put yourself in relation to it and then it becomes real in your world.

The two factors which are most important in my world, I would say, are my personality and then my relation to reality. Any real change in my personality should make a change in my outer world. I can interfere with the purely mechanical action of my brain by accepting what my brain does not register.

If I can imagine, then produce in myself a shift of personality and then it works, the One condition is imposed on man: that he believe that he already has that which he wishes. And one that confirms this: "When you stand praying, if you have aught against your brother, forgive him," etc.

You think this means to have something against someone? No. Forgiveness in the mystical sense tests man's ability to enter into and partake of the nature of the opposite. I think I cannot do something. That belief is what I must forgive. If I can do this, then I am forgiving myself.

If I can take a friend who is ill and accept the fact that he is ill, then I have that against him. I must forgive him by seeing him looking well, and to the degree that I am self-persuaded, I am forgiving what I held against him. Can you forgive a man by mumbling some words and saying you have forgiven him?

You can only forgive to the degree that "complete" change of consciousness takes place.

When I think of you, I should see a different you, a new you. If I do not see a different you then I have not forgiven you. This lady I told you of tonight "forgave" her friend, for she saw her happily married. And that marriage was consummated. I tell you that no matter what your dream is it can be realized, you will enact the crucifixion.

If you think the "resurrection is past already, you have departed from the truth" (II Timothy 2:18) It must be going on eternally. It is up to you what you do now. Everyone can do it. That is the purpose of this platform – so that you may not only realize your dreams here, but that you awaken and slip into other worlds.

There are worlds within this world, and worlds within worlds. I know – I have seen them and I have been in them. It does not matter what people say to me about whether I can do it or not. I know I can do it, and I do it.

I know that I live in a home in West LA. and come here on Monday and Thursday nights. You might as well tell me that I do not come here, as to say that I cannot enter some other sphere. I cannot take you with me, for the world only calls "reality" what can be shared. But it was not a subjective illusion; it was real.

There are many things that cannot be shared at the time, for the background of the other is not such that they are ready to receive it. But that does not make it less real. In time all will come to it.

CHAPTER 6

BY BLOOD & BY WATER

This lesson is taken from the First Epistle of John. Now these twenty-one letters, or Epistles, are not really addressed to individuals or groups. They are mysteries, as is the entire Bible.

Whether the Bible in the Old Testament tells the story in the form of history, or whether they tell it in the form of a parable, or in the form of a letter, they are all revelations of the mind of God, expressed in symbolism. Now, I do not claim that I can give you an exhaustive interpretation of any single story of the Bible. Because they are revelations of the mind of the Infinite, no single interpretation could ever be exhaustive.

On one level it may be true, and then you and I expand in consciousness and we re-read the letter and see it differently, and a further expansion in consciousness causes us, even when we re-read it for the third or fiftieth time, to still see the letter in a different light. So in this morning's interpretation I will try to keep it on to a level that is most practical.

We are told in this 5th chapter of First John, "This is He that came by water and blood even Jesus Christ, not by water only, but by water and blood." So these are symbols of birth. Every natural birth in the world is accompanied by the flowing of water and blood.

It's trying to tell the individual of a certain mystery of birth but he uses the word Christ Jesus and that is the symbol of a truly mysterious birth – something out of nothing. That is the mystery. Out of death life. Man cannot conceive it.

How can something alive come out of that which is dead – how can something come out of nothing? Man accepts it in the mineral world for he sees if he goes back far enough in time could he push the mystery in some remote past, he will accept the fact that some time, in a way not known to modern science, out of a non-organic substance came an organism.

He will call it by some little tiny name – an amoeba – and that will satisfy his mind, but he stops – he still will not admit that he stated that there was a non organic substance, or nothing or something that was dead, out of which came life – out of which came something.

He doesn't want to wrestle with that problem so he leaves that, jumps over the pages of history and comes to some little thing more complex. Then he teaches evolution from that state. But when he goes far enough back he finds no answer for the appearance of life out of nothing or death.

So here is the mystery. It comes by water and by blood, not by water only but by water and blood. This is the great mystery of the incarnation, the death and the resurrection. What incarnation – what death and what resurrection?

The mind instantly thinks in terms of two thousand years ago and we think that was the great mystery, but before I jump into the mystery, let me quote you the very last verse of this wonderful 5th chapter: "Little children keep yourselves from idols."

No matter how officialdom justifies them and tells you this is the image of your Savior revealed through the minds of a Saint or a great artist, you are warned in this chapter to keep yourselves free, completely free of idols, in harmony with the Second Commandment, "Thou shall make no graven image unto the Lord thy God."

No matter how it is justified by officialdom or orthodox society, you are asked please not to make anything external to your own mind and bow before it as a creative power, for here he is trying to reveal the true creative power that is in man.

It sleeps in man as his passive mind. As you unfold the mystery, it awakens from its passive state into its active state, and the birth of the active mind is truly the resurrection of Christ in man. It is Christ in man that is the hope of glory.

Now here in another verse, he gives you a test. He asks you to ask whatsoever thing in this world in My Name that the Father may give it you. He did not restrict you to one desire – ask whatsoever thing you desire in my name and the Father may give it you.

Now, if you take it literally, as I have heard thousands and thousands of prayers in my own home, - raised in a Christian atmosphere – we said grace at meals and Mother invariably said it and invariably ended with the words "For Jesus' sake, Amen" but nothing happened.

We ate the food and enjoyed the food, and you will say prayers – long verbal appeals to God for something always ending "For Jesus' sake, Amen", thinking that if I said it was for His sake that I would so tempt my Father to give it to me, for did he not say:

"Whatsoever thing ye desire, ask it in My name, and the Father will give it to you." Well, you ask it forever in that name and nothing happens – therefore, he didn't understand the mystery – so what is the mystery – even Jesus Christ who came not by water only, but by water and the blood.

We have put it into the most practical manner in the world – something out of nothing – life out of death. Conceive of something you desire. Just think of it. The mere thinking of something, that is a conception unaided by another. Is that not an "immaculate conception?"

You knew no one in the formulation of your desire. Now you intend to realize it. It is clear in your mind's eye – it is a holy conception – it is a virgin conception. Can you bring about that something that seemingly is not existing – it is non-existent – it has no existence in fact, and embody it? Can you incarnate it? For this is the mystery of the incarnation that comes by water and blood.

Here is a birth that could take place if I am willing to give it human parentage. I must give it human parentage – it cannot of itself be born, for unless I myself become it, it cannot be born; so I desire to be something other than what I am.

Now what is the water? The water is the great mystery, the great psychological truth that I must discover which will enable me, if I accept it to live a life according to that truth and give expression to my desire. For water is the truth and the blood is the application of that truth. I could know everything in the world to be known of the mystery but never live by it; still continue to live as I have always lived, passively, accepting the evidence of my senses as fact.

Accepting the dictates of reason as my guide; I could overhear a conversation or I could read it in a book, or hear it in a place like this on a Sunday morning – that if you desire something intensely and you truly desire it, and you have a clear mental picture of what you would like to be or what you would like to accomplish, or what you would like another friend to realize – you know exactly what you would like in this world.

Now, this is the water by which it could be born, but it cannot be born of water only, it must be born of water and blood, so I will give you the water: when you know what you want, you make as vivid and as lifelike a representation of what you would see, of what you would hear and what you would do were you physically present and physically moving about in such a situation.

To take an example – suppose I desired a certain apartment or a certain home or a certain business. Take one, so you will not be confused. We will take an apartment. But reason tells me I cannot afford it. Reason tells me I haven't enough furniture for so big an apartment – reason tells me a thousand things that would deny that I could ever realize it, but I still would like it.

Now this is what I would give you in the form of water for something must come out of nothing and life out of death. To embody that state I make it real. You pull it seemingly from a state that is non-existent; therefore, something out of nothing. To make it real and to incarnate it and to become alive to it and it to you, you are pulling life out of death.

Now this is what you do. There is a death involved but it is not the kind of death that men call death. There is a death – there is a radical change of your state of mind. You completely give up the belief that you are not living in such a place; that is irrational, but that is what you are called upon to do; to completely deny the evidence of your senses and to boldly assume that you are already in that state that you occupy.

There you dwell in a state that reason denies. You dwell in an assumption that your senses deny. That is just the water. If you do it, you are applying the blood. If you are told to do it, you are given the truth, for it will work. That water, if you could only add the blood to it, will bring the invisible state into the visible world, and what seemingly is non-existent will crystallize and harden into fact.

But if you only know it, as too many of us know it, and think the mere knowledge is enough – we will come here on Sunday morning and thoroughly enjoy this wonderful hour – the music, the message, the meditation, the feeling of companionship you find here, and the whole thing is a thrill for an hour – but such knowledge cannot bring Christ Jesus to birth.

In this state Christ Jesus, – now, I'll analyze it for you, – on a lower plane the word Jesus means salvation; the word Jesus, which is Jeshua, means to save. If I desire something and I don't realize it, then I simply continue a life of frustration.

If I realize my objective, I have been saved from frustration. Take a simple matter. Suppose I wanted a suit of clothes because I was in need of raiment. If I don't realize the suit of clothes I am not saved from my nudity. If I realize the suit of clothes, I have been saved. For this is an all inclusive Savior, not just a man.

If I wanted water, literal water, a lecture will not quench my thirst. If I wanted food, literal food, the most wonderful revelation would not actually satisfy my hunger, so Jesus is all inclusive, meaning everything you desire. He is it, because if you embodied that desire, you embodied your Jesus.

Now, to embody Jesus; He cannot be embodied by the knowledge of what to do only. He can only be embodied by the application of that knowledge. So the knowledge of what to do is called water; the water of Truth; but the use of that lovingly is called the flowing of the blood.

So here we find the symbols that always accompany birth, that which is presented in this mystery. You are told the limit is within you. You make the limit. There is no limit. Whatsoever you desire, ask in My name, for name simply means nature. If I wanted to be in a house and to feel that I am the occupant of that house, there is a certain feeling, a certain nature that goes with it. I must appropriate it as though it were true.

Here I am called upon to bring something alive out of a state that is dead. If I told you what I have done, you would question my sanity and you would feel I am trying to give expression to something that is being pulled out of nothing. This is because you cannot see it. You don't see me in the house.

You don't see me actually occupying and enjoying the life that you know I desire to enjoy, so if I persist in that assumption, to you, - if you should know my persistency, - you might think I am headed towards a form of insanity, but if tomorrow the house becomes an embodied fact and I the occupant, then you look at it passively – you will still try to justify it by tracing its appearance back to a visible cause.

You will see that in some way, unknown to you, my resources were lifted up, that in some way I became more eligible for that house and you will trace it back to a change in my fortune, you will trace it back to a change in something in my world, but you won't trace these changes back to the unseen assumption in which I dwell.

So, as the mystic tells us in the 11th of his Letters to the Hebrews: "'Things seen were not made of things that do appear." Man refuses to accept it so he takes everything in his world and tries to take it back to some visible cause, even with the aid of his microscope.

He takes the microscope and he will peer through it to prove to his own satisfaction there is a visible, tangible cause; or he goes off into space with his telescope. He must find in the outer world causes of the changes in the outer world.

He cannot believe that the whole vast outer world is held together from within and we are only on the surface looking at it from without and trying to analyze it and to understand it from without, and all that appears without, though it seems there, it isn't. It is all from within – all within the mind of man – and that is the mystery.

So do not make an idol, no matter who makes you the idol, no matter what holy man tells you this is a wonderful thing that will bless you – there is no blessing in states on the outside. Bow to nothing on the outside.

We have wondered why throughout the centuries a certain race of people did not become greater sculptors, greater artists in the form of painting great religious teachers. Maybe they were really taking that second commandment very, very seriously. Make no graven image, no not one, unto Me. Make nothing that is graven, that is objective, as an image of your Father that is free, for I AM Spirit.

If you were to worship Me you worship Me in spirit and in truth but not in anything that you can turn to on the outside and bend the knee before it, whether it be a church, a synagogue, or some statue that hangs upon your wall, He is not there, He is in your mind; He is housed within you – there is the living

God within the Temple and the temple is man. "Ye are the temple of the living God."

So when I speak of the water and the blood I speak not of the things that you can see with the eye, such as water, and such as blood. They are only symbolized functions of the mind and the function first comes with water.

I must first know what to do before I can do it. So water comes first. He takes water and puts it into a stone jar, gives it something like a shape, and from that stone jar filled with water He draws not water; He converts it, He draws wine.

So here is the first miracle. I know what to do. I take this little world of mine that is stone and then I extract from it something that is not seen, not quite as hard as that. I call it water. I see something bringing all this into being. I know how it's brought into being.

That a man living in luxury is not to be judged harshly because he has it and you haven't it. He is living in a state of consciousness that solidifies in the form that you see now and call luxurious, one in a state of health, one who is recognized, one who is accomplished, one who is contributing much to the world. Don't judge them.

These are states made visible. Find out if you can get into a similar state. He is not occupying the only state in the world. There are infinite states and if you try even to duplicate that state, it can be duplicated, or you can get close to it or you can transcend it.

Find out within your own mind's eye what you want. Don't be envious of him. Leave him alone for he is applying the law: he is entitled to everything in this world that he can actually conceive and desire and put himself into and live it for man is living in an infinite world of invisible states and an individual wisely or foolishly occupies a state.

While he remains faithful to the state, the state will externalize and become the circumstances and the conditions of his life. The moment he detaches himself in consciousness from that state the things that he enjoyed before vanish from his world.

Now, if everything in my world depends upon a state of consciousness, it would be the height of insanity to seek the thing before I actually fix within myself the state on which the thing depends, for that which requires a state of consciousness to produce its effect cannot be effected without such a state of consciousness, so when I know what I want, to support that, there is an invisible state of consciousness.

The world calls that invisible state a non-existing nothingness. They cannot even call it a thing for to them it has no existence, no reality. That is the mystery – a self begotten child conceived unaided by another and carried faithfully in the womb of God, which is the mind of man; it was placed there without the aid of another, by man's desire. That was the immaculate concept, that's the virgin conception.

Now the virgin birth; can I bring it from its invisible state and really make it a tangible fact within my world? Try it! As you try it with one thing, and you succeed, you will try it with two and four and eight and so on, and eventually the sleeping giant in man, which is the son of God in man called Christ, will awaken. He will awaken by moving from the passive state to the active state.

The passive state is simply the complete and utter surrender of man to appearances; to live believing that life is on the outside, and he moves from that state where he surrenders and believes all these things to be causes to the active state where he puts everything in subjection to that something within himself which is his awakened imagination.

He imagines a thing to be so, he persuades himself that it is so and walks faithful to his assumption. Then you will know why in the 14th of the Letters to Romans he tells us that every man be fully persuaded in his own mind – don't persuade her, leave her alone – you persuade yourself of the changes you desire expressed in her.

If you desire a change in your relationships at home or in business, you don't argue, you don't persuade them, for let every man be fully persuaded in his own mind; so can I persuade myself that you are as I desire to see you? Then, to the degree that I can persuade myself, you will conform in the outer world to that persuasion.

If I hope to see changes there, before I myself will start the change on the inside, the chances are I will hope in vain. You, yourself, may desire certain changes and I might see them change in my world, but they were not caused because I moved into an active state.

I am still reflective and most of us in this world are reflecting life, and the purpose of a church of this nature is to make us not reflect but to affect life. If I affect it then Christ is awakened within me. If I only reflect it, then I sleep with Adam, and the purpose is to move from the sleep of Adam to the wakefulness of the son of God, called Christ.

Adam, too, is called the son of God but in the state of profound sleep, but he moves from that state of sleep, or the passive state of the mind, to the active state and is then called Christ Jesus. But such cannot be born by the knowledge of what to do alone. It can only be born by such knowledge applied.

So if I take even a little bit, if I never came here again and took what I have heard this morning, that little bit of knowledge, if applied, will be far more fruitful than much knowledge which I gather Sunday after Sunday which is not applied.

So if you have all the water in the world – by water I mean spiritual truths – you didn't ever apply them, then you will be no nearer the proving of it than you are now; but if you took a little bit, one drop of this water, and went out even to disprove it, but in order to disprove it, you must seriously and sincerely try it.

If you try it, you won't disprove it, you will be encouraged to drink more water and still more and bring about this birth of your Savior; and you decide what will save you today from your present predicament. It may be a job.

It may be an increase of funds, it may be companionship. It may be something I don't know, but whatever it is that you this day desire, and unless you get it you feel thwarted – you feel frustrated –

then it would save you if you got it. Now take that as your Savior. Look into your mind's eye and see it clearly.

It may seem almost sacrilegious to the orthodox mind to tell you that when you see clearly in your mind's eye the state desired, either for self or another, you are actually looking into the face of Jesus, for you are seeing the state that could save you from where you are or what you are.

So you try it, and the mind will expand. You will find yourself not only increasing in this world, in the outer world, but you will find mystical revelations taking place within you, which is the purpose of the teaching.

It is not just to bring about changes in the outer world that are desirable but to bring about changes in the inner that ascends man on higher levels of consciousness – for the purpose of the whole appearance of man is to awaken from the lowest descent on the ladder to the highest.

He is ascending to the highest, for we are told in the vision of Jacob, above it all stood God, on the ladder stood these heavenly beings ascending and descending but above all stood God, so the real destiny of man is to reach the height that he may awaken as God.

So the mystery is God became man that man may become God – so He came down as man. Take the same verse and give it a higher interpretation. So here God died yes, to become man. The death of God is complete forgetfulness of the fact that He is God.

He had to completely forget that He is God, and therefore die to awaken as man. If he remembered He was God He just couldn't be man, but a complete and utter death, which is complete forgetfulness, that I am God, to become man.

So the poet wrote it beautifully and said, God became man that man may become God. Then he asked unless I die you could not live, but if I die I shall arise again and you with me. Then he goes on to ask man, could you love one who had never died for thee?

Or: could you die for one who had not died for thee? So he is putting this into the most wonderful poetical mystery in the book Jerusalem, by Blake; so he reveals to the mind who can see it, that you who believe yourself because you are visible and you must do what man passively must do: he traces your origin back to a germ.

As long as you began as a germ, you are no more than a big germ. If you begin as something else you are only something enlarged of the same thing. For all ends run true to origins. If I can take you back where you cannot see it and take you back to the great mystery that you are actually begotten of God, if your origin is God, your end is God.

If your origin is a bug then your end is a bug – so you have the choice, passive mind, which is really the scientific mind, must still insist on finding causes external to itself. It cannot find causes in that passive state within itself. I tell you the great mystery is that you came out of a seeming death. It is a death. God died to become man, because He desired the companionship of men as Gods, as the poet told us, "Man should not stay a man.

His aim should higher be. For God will only Gods accept, as company." So you cannot in your present state of the passive mind be companions of your Father who longs and desires that every son, every child. Awakens to become companions of Deity.

So to do it, He had to die as God, and become His creation in the hope that the creation would awaken and become His companion. But you see He gave us such a gift. He completely freed me of the responsibility of returning. I don't have to awaken. I am as free as the wind.

He gave me complete freedom of will. I may hurt myself, ruin myself, but because of the gift of God to me, to make me alive. He cannot interfere and cause me to awaken. He may appeal through awakened children and they may appeal to their sleeping brother, but they cannot by the same law interfere with the will of the sleeping brother.

No matter who awakes they cannot interfere and make me awake. They can only appeal and try in some subtle way to suggest, but the gift was absolute.

God gave Himself to become me, and finding myself man, I think my origin was man, so my destiny, no matter how big a man I become, no matter how wise a man, it will still be a man. But if my origin is God, my destiny is God and I will awaken one day to discover this wonderful unfolding mystery within myself.

CHAPTER 7

THE BREAD & THE WINE

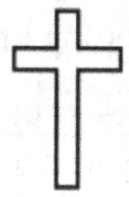

When we say that the supreme power that created the universe is the same power that is resident in man, people question that statement. Possibly everyone here owns a Bible, and when you go to court as a witness – say you are called to swear that you will tell the truth – and to swear you put your hand on the Bible, or the Word of God.

Then you open the Bible and read: "Whatsoever things you desire, believe that you have them...and you shall receive them. And when you stand praying, forgive, if you have aught against your brother, so that your Father in heaven may even so forgive you."

You put your hand on the book of truth and swear to tell the truth, and here is this statement in this very book on which you swear, and you don't believe it.

It is true. It is based on the statement: Imagination creates reality, for the Bible is addressed to the real man, Imagination. "For the Eternal body of man is The Imagination; that is God himself." (Blake)

Is there anything you cannot imagine? Yet many cannot believe what the Book says is true. You admit you can imagine it, yet man does not believe that the thing imagined can be true. But I tell you that if you can imagine it and persist, your persistence will win and you will prove the truth of that statement in Mark 11 given above.

However, that is on this level of the world. It is called in the Bible "feasting on the bread and fish," or the loaves and fishes. We can bring about all the changes we desire in our world if we imagine we have it and persist in that state, for if I will persist I will win. But there is another diet spoken of in the Bible and it is called "bread and wine."

You can go and get all the things of the world with the bread and fish, and you are invited to feast on it if you wish, but the other diet does something to a man that not one in a billion would believe. We are told that they despaired, for they could not believe it. They were told regarding this second diet: "If you eat it and drink it you do it in remembrance of me."

Who? The one who is called Jesus Christ in the Bible, or the spirit of forgiveness. You must feast on this, and it has nothing to do with a cup of wine or a little wafer. It is "the spirit of forgiveness." It is "the mutual point of forgiveness between enemies, the birthplace of the Lamb of God." And throughout eternity I forgive you and you forgive me, and just as he said: "This is the wine and this is the bread."

So if I know how to eat of that bread and drink of that wine I am forgiving every person in the world. But I cannot do it unless I see and understand the difference between an individual and the state the individual is occupying. If I condemn a man, or a society, or a thing, and I do not understand that they are only states, I am condemning them.

Only when I begin to distinguish between the state and the individual can I forgive. Then I can take the most horrible beast in the world and embrace him. He might in this present state be my worst enemy, but if I know he is only in a state, I can take him mentally and embrace him and pull him out of that state into which he has fallen and put him into a nobler state. And that is the "point of mutual forgiveness between enemies, the birthplace of the Lamb of God."

So when man will eat this bread and drink this wine he can have anything there is, for there is only One, for the whole is given to us, if we know it. If any man gives you anything he gives you what is mine as well as yours, for everything is given to you and to me. All is ours. We are one.

Get things if you want them. But there is something far beyond the mere getting of things. But if you want [to] imagine things, they are here. Do not deny yourself anything you desire, unless you would be gaining by another's alleged loss. That is not the way to do it. You do not take from anyone.

You create what you desire only in Imagination, and if you persist in the state it will prove itself, and it will come to you in a way that will not hurt another, for it is my Father who is giving it to me. There is only God.

Nothing is lost, for "all things by a law divine with one another's being mingle." So I do not have to ask you or another to play your part in bringing to pass what I want in this world. If you are relative to my drama you will be drawn into it. All I must do is eat of the bread and fish.

But there is the other diet, the bread and the wine. Then when I meet someone I call enemy I must know that he is in a state, and I must distinguish between the individual and the state into which he has fallen. For it is really God in the state. There is only God to play every part. So I can embrace that being I call my enemy and have him see in me his most interested friend. So I redeem him.

That is the wine and the bread, and if I eat of the bread and drink of the wine I will actually give birth to the Lamb of God. What must I do to bring about this experience? It will not come to anyone unless he eats this bread and drinks this wine, for that is the unconditional forgiveness of sin.

No matter what the person has ever done, if you can distinguish between the individual and the state into which that individual has fallen, you can embrace him, and then you prepare the way for the birth of the Lamb of God.

If you feel you cannot do it yet, then try the other diet. It is wonderful.

If you want better health, or a finer job, or a larger world, then you use Imagination to create it. You hear and see and touch as if your dream were a reality, and then you persist, and with persistence you will win.

If you will only persist in hearing and in seeing what you want to see, you cannot fail to realize it. It is a wonderful diet, and everyone is invited to feast upon it. "Whatsoever things you desire, when you pray believe that you have them, and you shall have them." You need no other on the outside, but if you will have anything against another forgive him and your Father will forgive you.

Some pious monk added the last part, which is now deleted from the newer, more accurate version of the Bible: "If you don't forgive, then your Father will not forgive you." That was not the original text. There is no punishment, no retribution. It is all up to us.

We are walking through this fire which is called Earth, but if man only knows that these are states, he will understand that the spirit is walking as God, walking as the Son of God. Then it is the God we embrace, but man cannot believe it and he worships another, unknown God.

Everyone who walks the face of this Earth is God, but there are unnumbered states created for a purpose, and we can use our minds to take anyone from an unlovely state.

You recall the recent discussion regarding juvenile delinquents. They could all be put away, we are told.

The judge does not know that he could do something about it instead of just corralling them and putting them on the backs of the taxpayers.

If the judge only knew that this being before him is in a state, and that he could create a new state and bring that being into a new state and enable him to become a noble wonderful being in society! But we cannot see that, so we continue to condemn the individual as the state.

No one can feast on the bread and wine until he can see that, and then he can reach the place of mutual forgiveness of enemies, the birthplace of the Lamb of God. "So spoke the merciful Son of Heaven to those whose Western Gates were open, but sleeping humanity heard him not, and slumbered on."

Only those whose Western Gates were open heard it. [And] those go forward to create new states for another and so he saves himself, for man is saved by (and only by) the saving of his fellow man.

Finally in each the Western Gate opens and then the Lamb of God is born. A good Catholic friend said to me: "What do you do to have this experience?" And I said, "Drink the wine and eat the bread." He did not understand, for he takes Communion every Sunday.

I said: "Has anything happened to you? Has there been an expansion in your consciousness? You have taken it for these many years." But that is not the bread or wine I mean.

The wine is mutual forgiveness of all enmity throughout eternity, just as the dear Savior said. If I cannot embrace a being and feel myself thrill to his good fortune, I have not taken the wine or the bread. But if I do it within and not by taking something in a tangible form, then I have partaken of the true bread and wine, and we have schoolrooms within schoolrooms.

It does not matter who you are or when you were born; that has nothing to do with the awakening of God in man. Who are the "right" people? Everyone is God.

I had a long distance call yesterday from New York. The lady who called me is very, very rich by the standards of diamonds and money. She has not fingers enough for all her diamonds. She has everything she wants − except one thing: she wants to be happily married to someone in the social register who has more money than she has, and is at least twenty years younger.

She is seventy-five, but she wants more money and bigger diamonds. She said to me: "Look what I have done for my son by using this law. He can now send his four girls to private school. I did this for him when I persisted. But I cannot seem to bring this picture for myself into being."

I said: "Anything you can imagine you can create. But you are thinking the market is limited because there are so few in the register or in your social sphere. Everyone walking the Earth is God and there is no greater background than that. These people are only in states, and if you took them out of that state you might not care for them at all – the same being, but another state.

You do not distinguish the being from the state. You used this same law to put your son where he now is. You can realize your dream of being married to someone richer and younger than you are, if that is your concept." It is not mine.

We judge no one, for when you awaken you do not see the state. You only see the individual who has fallen into the state, and when you see that, you do not meet anyone you could not embrace and pull out of an unlovely state and put him into another state. Then we can intermingle as one being.

Now, he may go back into the old state, like Lot's wife. "How many times must I do it, Lord?" "Seventy times seven." That is how it is.

If a child of yours fell downstairs, would you not pick him up seventy times seven? God is playing all the parts. There are unnumbered schools teaching that you suffer because of something you did in a previous life. You must do this or that.

You do not awaken by sitting on a mountaintop, or by diets, or by joining some "ism." You can only awake as you eat the bread and drink the wine, for that is the mutual forgiveness of enemies, and that place is the birthplace of the Lamb of God. You do not say to another: "I forgive you."

That means nothing. But you bring him before your mind's eye and embrace him. You are in states that seem to oppose, but when you feel that touch, you are opening the Western Gate, for the Western Gate is touch. The Southern Gate is sight. The Eastern Gate is scent.

The whole world remains asleep because the Western Gate is [closed] in you. And then you eat of this bread. You touch the one you embrace. Embrace mentally the very one who would cut off your head. Then the Western Gate is open in you, and then you eat this bread and drink of this wine, and then you prepare it.

It is not by joining any orthodox church or going on some diet. You can sit on the Himalayas until you freeze and cannot do it. But you walk the market-place and mingle with God (which is man) and then you have unnumbered opportunities every day to eat this bread and drink this wine.

Distinguish between the individual and the state he is in. You have never been tarnished.

Hitler, you say? Stalin? The states were horrible, but the individual has never been touched. We do not give birth to the Lamb of God by condemnation. We must reach the point of mutual forgiveness of enemies, the birthplace of the Lamb of God.

Then everything begins to unfold and you will know and understand that everything said in the Book is being said about you. There is only the one Son, and God is begetting that Son unceasingly from you and from me forever.

If you want the Son to be born in you, you must practice drinking the wine; or, if you want to, feed on the bread and the fish. Bring before your mind's eye your world as you want it. Hear, touch, see, and feel what you would if your desire were true, and you will change your world in harmony with that im-age. You can make it conform to your image, but be-yond that are worlds within worlds.

This universe, which seems so vast — a million light years in diameter — is only the skin of a greater world, for there are endless worlds within worlds. So when God created me and lit me, therefore I pre-dated the thing created. So before the world was I AM. I begin then to remember who I am and I am He, for God and man are one.

We awaken by drinking the wine and eating the bread. You can practice it all day long. You do not leave where you are or go anywhere to do it. You can do it standing in a bar. It has nothing to do with moral virtues. These are only states.

Then you will understand the words of Paul: "Drink no longer water, but use a little wine for thy stom-ach's sake." "Water" is psychological truth. Stop simply absorbing it and begin to put into practice what you know; that is turning the water into wine.

It's the first great miracle in the Bible. No more just reading and not practicing. I can absorb the water, but now I must take a little wine – or put into practice what I have heard and so transform your world – and that is life. The 11th chapter of Mark is true: "Whatsoever you desire, when you pray believe that you have it, and you shall receive it."

"And as you stand praying if you have aught against your brother, forgive him, that your Father may for-give you." But you cannot forgive until you distinguish between the state, and the individual in the state.

You create for him that other state, where he is your friend, bring him out of his former state, and embrace him. That is the opening the Western Gate – and then something happens within you. So, who spoke this?

"The merciful Son of Heaven to those whose Western Gate was open, but sleeping humanity heard him not and slumbered on." [Blake.] I can speak and you may not hear. This diet may not appeal to you. It is only a state which you are in at present, for you are still God, no matter what, and you are still unblemished. But all will awaken, for God plays all the parts.

Therefore "disaster beyond redemption is impossible." Let no one tell you that you are better than the other. You may be in a more wonderful state than the other, but that is all. Good and evil belong to the tree of knowledge. We are rising up to a more expanding world as we awaken.

You will step into another world as real as this one, and yet behind you in this world you [will] discover you have left a little garment – your body. All things exist in Imagination, and it is one with the supreme imagining that creates and sustains the universe.

Now, you take the diet you desire. If you are not yet interested in embracing someone you think is your opponent, and all you want is to transcend your present level, then live in the state that proves you have done it. You may never, after it comes about, give credit to your wonderful Imagination, for it happens so naturally that you will think it would have happened anyway.

You may discount that your Imagination did it. But the day will come when you will want to transcend just things, and you will want that which does not have earthly value. You will see those with great possessions and know they are actually only moments from the grave, but up to the last second before they flicker out they are still only conscious of possessions.

But it is all right, for they too will awaken in time, though they do not even know that there is someone who walks among them who is awake. In the world beyond worlds you are completely awake and not known because of possessions – because then you own the world. For there you know that you and your Father are one, and he creates all out of nothing.

Whatever you desire to create you create, and you do not need atoms to do it; forever those you create out of your Imagination. But tonight bring a friend (or he may be an opponent) before your mind's eye and represent him to yourself as being in a finer state, or freer, and then be faithful to your mental structure. Then, in a way no one knows, it will take on reality in your world and crystallize and become a fact.

CHAPTER 8

THE ART OF DYING

If you are with us for the first time, this is what we believe and teach here. We firmly believe that you, the individual, can realize your every dream, and the reason is that God and man are one. We believe that the difference is not in the mentality with which we operate, but only in the degrees of intensity of the operant power itself, and that we call human imagination.

Keats said: "You can take any one great and spiritual passage and it will serve as a starting point to lead you to the two-and-thirty palaces." Take this simple one in Paul's letters to the Corinthians: "I die daily," or Blake's statement in his letter to Crab Robinson: "Death is the best thing in life.

There is nothing in life like death, but people take such a long time in dying. At least, their neighbors never see them rise from the grave."

If you understood Blake you would not think of death as the world thinks of death, but you would see that no one can grow without outgrowing. But man is not willing to outgrow, [and] yet he wants other things than those he has. But if you remain in one state, you will forever have to suffer the consequences of not being in another state. (From the "Hermetica")

If I remain in the state of poverty, I must suffer the consequences of not being in the state of wealth. So I must learn the art of dying. Paul says: "I die daily."

Blake says: "People take such a long time in dying." Man does not outgrow his state of ill health or his old job or his environment. We must learn the art of dying, and this week is the great death and we are told that God dies that man may live.

We say that the Imagination of God and man are one, no matter how far it goes. Universes are created and sustained by "the same power that sustains our environment." We say the power is the same, but we recognize a vast difference between the power that sustains the universe and that which sustains an environment.

The difference is only is in the degree of intensity of the center of imagining. So, if we increase the intensity in the center of imagining, we will create greater and greater things. So I see my dream, and I must learn to die to what I AM in order to live to what I want to be.

Now this is the mystical meaning of a death in the Bible − the death of Moses, a story familiar to all of us. We are told that Moses comes out of the land of Moab (Deuteronomy 34) and then scales the mountain of Nebo, goes to Pisgah, sees Gilead, and finally he looks into the promised land of Jericho.

But the Lord tells him: "I will let you see the land, but you cannot go into it." Then Moses dies. (The present state cannot be carried into the new; it has to die as a consequence of the new made alive.) "But his eye was not dim and his natural force was not abated." And no one knows his burial place.

First remember that all the characters of the Bible take place in the mind of man. I am Moses, you are Moses. It means to "lift up" or to "draw out of." We are told in the very beginning of the story that he was pulled from the bulrushes. The word ["Moses" - in Hebrew, "Moshe"] spelled backwards in the ancient Hebrew means "the Name" [haShem] or "I AM."

So I am drawing out of my own being, or the I AM. Moses comes from "Mo ab." This comes from two Hebrew words meaning "Mother-Father," or "womb." Then he scales the mount of Nebo, which means "to prophesy," or which represents the subjective state I long for. I will prophesy for you, or you for another. You single out a person's longing.

If he longs for something it means that he does not have it, else there could be no longing. But Moses climbs Nebo — that is, he participates in seeing the state longed for. I single out something that implies I am the man I want to be. I scale the mountain. Then comes Pisgah, which means, "to contemplate."

I contemplate what I want to be. Then he sees Jericho, which means "a fragrant odor." I will contemplate the desired state until I get the feeling or reaction that satisfies. I have not only scaled Nebo but I have reached Pisgah and looked into Jericho.

I am filled with the emotion that implies the act is completed. Then there is Gilead, which means, "hills of witnesses." Then I, as Moses, die. I cannot go into the promised land, and no one can find where I am buried.

What does it mean? If I am poverty-ridden and frightened and then you meet me and see me as free as a bird and happy, then I am not the man you knew who was frightened. Then where is that other man buried?

For Moses is the power in man (generic man, male-female) to draw out of himself anything in this world he desires, and to so enact the drama that he dies to what he was, that he may live to what he is enacting. That is Moses – and no one can know where he is buried.

But we are told: "His eye was not dim nor his natural force abated." That is [to say], when I die, that is when I enact the drama. I do not wait for signs to appear; it is when I am most aware of my restrictions and feel the pressures, then is when I must learn to die.

I must learn to let go of what my senses dictate and "go mad" and yield to what is only a dream. But sustaining it and living in it, I die to what was physically real as I gradually lift up what was only the dream. You knew only the frightened man and not the other one. No one can tell where the other has gone.

So this is how the art of dying is dramatized in the Bible as the death of a man. But it has nothing to do with any certain man, for the story of the Bible takes place in the mind of every man. I will crucify myself, for God crucified himself in me that I might live.

But now I must nail myself upon the thing I desire and, remaining faithful to it, lift it up as God nailed himself upon me. (The present body) is believing himself a man called Neville, giving Neville the same power that is his (but keyed low) in the hope that I will lift up the power to bigger things in my world to which I can nail myself, and so lift them up.

There is no possibility of man making his dream alive unless He nails himself to this cross that is man. We are living because God nailed himself to us. Now man, keyed low, yielding to other states and not to what the senses dictate, becomes one with the state and nails himself to it (fixes himself in the state through emotion and feeling) and then he will be lifted up.

For crucifixion comes before resurrection. Crucifixion without resurrection would be unthinkable; it would be the utter triumph of tyranny. If I could yield myself to my dream and it would not become flesh, it would be complete tyranny over this wonderful concept of life. But you cannot fail if you yield.

If you hold back within yourself, wondering "What will I play as my last card if this doesn't work?" then you have not yielded, you have not nailed yourself to it. It is a complete yielding. It is the great cry "My God! My God! Why hast Thou forsaken me?"

If you know that you're God doing it, you can yield. But there must be complete abandonment as though it were true and then you make it a reality. The cost is that form of mental abandonment that Blake calls "madness." But man is afraid; he dare not so abandon himself to a dream, and so never "dies." So Blake was right when he said: "There is nothing like death: the best thing in life is death."

Many people only age, but never change inwardly. They only mature physically, but they have not died in the mystical sense. There is no transforming power in the physical death, and they will still be anchored in a larger world with all the trends of this world. To our senses they seem to be dead but they will still, on another plane, have to learn the art of dying.

I can anywhere so completely detach myself from what is taking place that I can "die" to that state. So every little death is the lifting of the divine image. This means dying as the mystic means it. It means dying mentally. Man dies to ill health, or poverty, or to disharmony, etc., but he does it by yielding to the other states.

Blake looks on all states as permanent, as in his great poem regarding the Halls of Los: "I curse the earth for man and made it permanent." So states remain and man passes through states, as though cities.

If I do not pass through some state but remain in it, I think it is the only reality. You cannot conceive of a state that is not, for the whole is finished; but man is awakening only by dying to state after state.

You take a friend who is not well or cannot set himself free from some state. You represent that friend to yourself as he should be seen by the whole world, and to the degree that you are faithful to that representation, to that degree you will bring him out of the old state.

It does not matter if he knows you did it or not; he does not have to know. But remain faithful and you will bring him out of the old state into the new state that you are seeing.

All things are burned up when we cease to behold them. Moses could see the promised land but he could not go into it. If I am true to the likeness of what I behold, then I – the "old" man – cannot go into the new state. Something called the power goes into it, but no one recognizes it, for they cannot recognize the transformed being. We all feel so secure in recurrence.

If we know that a thing is fixed and that next week things will be as they are today, I feel secure in that recurrence. I can have done something that violates the moral codes, I can have come from the wrong side of the tracks, but I can accept that, for I am used to it. But to say that something awakes in me and can become what it will − that is frightening to man. So we are told to awake out of sleep, for recurrence brings security to the whole vast world.

One does what he does as if he did it in a nightmare. For God had to "forget" he was God to become man, and that whittling down to this level is the very limit of contraction, But then comes the awakening from that deep dream into which he threw himself to make me alive. So this lifting-up power goes about setting men free, for God became every man, that every man may in time awaken as God.

Eventually the whole world will awaken and the poem will be in full bloom and it will be noble beyond our wildest dreams. And then it will exist for us and we will be one with the creator of the great poem. That is the art of dying.

Next Sunday is the great drama. I am riding a beast and I am at the crossroads. "Bring me a colt on which no man ever sat, that is tied by the road where two ways meet." Here is state I have never ridden before. It is so unnatural to feel myself to be the man I want to be and to actually get into that state and ride it without being thrown by reason, which tells me I am mad.

But if you know the Lord is your Imagination, you can ride it into Jerusalem. We are told we will find the animal at a crossroads where two roads meet. We are always at a crossroads of what I am and what I want to be. So, can I ride the beast I find at the crossroads and ride it into Jerusalem? Then I am going toward "heaven," but it is not continuous on my line of motion. It is contiguous.

It is adjacent to where I am, for heaven is a state of consciousness. I try to catch the feeling that would be mine if I were the man I want to be, but that involves a death. I must abandon myself to my dream as if it were true, and − living in it − I lift it up and make it real.

Everyone must pass through this state, for this is the only true religion in the world. Religion, like charity, begins at home, with one's self. The mother seed of all religious beliefs lies in the mystical experiences of the individual. All ceremonies are but secondary growths superimposed upon it.

Religion means, "to be tied or devoted to." But if I am not in love with what I am tied to, I must yield to something more lovely and make it real. I must bear my cross. I go so far and then I want to cross to the other line where my heaven is. For everything is interrelated. We all interpenetrate each other. We are all one.

So there is interpenetration of the whole world and then comes conflict, and from that comes the solution of the conflict. For we must conflict if we are all interpenetrated. But then we must bring about reconciliation. Whatever the solution is, that is the reconciliation. But we cannot stay in a state or any condition forever. Each new state bears within it the seeds of new conflict.

Every heaven becomes in time hell. A thing is ours for a moment, but as we continue in it, it will bring about conflict. As long as there is interpenetration there is always conflict. So live in any desired state and then as conflict arises resolve it and die to it and then move into another state. Thus we grow and outgrow; thus man awakes.

No man can be born in one environment and ever realize another if he does not yield to the state desired. So Blake was right: "The best thing in life is death but it takes man so long to die that his friends never see him rise from the grave."

Can you not see then how it is with your friend who always tells you the same things, even though you have not seen him for ten years? Everything is still recurring, nothing is new, but that makes him feel secure. Man does not want change; it frightens him.

I tell you that your Imagination is God. Believe it. Exercise it. It is keyed low, but as you lift it up you intensify it and then vision after vision will be yours as you begin to awake. Do not think you are greedy because you are demanding things or the changing of things.

You are here to create as your Father creates. Want what you want and yield to it and create it. Then you will want higher and higher things. But nothing blesses a man unless it comes down from its heavenly state and takes on flesh. You are the only one who can clothe it in reality. But it remains a state unless you yield to it.

This drama in the Bible is all about you, for the Christ Jesus of the gospels is your own wonderful Imagination. There is only an infinite God and the creation he loved. And he so loved it, he wanted to make it alive and then share it and even change it, so God became man that man may become God. That is the great story of the gospels.

Every mystic in the world tells this same story. Then every man is free. There is no judgment, for no matter what man has done, it is God's doing it in a nightmare. There is only complete forgiveness of sin – no judgment and no argument, but man can change facts. The past can be unmade. So a man has done this or that. Use your strange Imagination and "turn the great wheel backward until Troy unburns." It means to revise.

I know a lady who burned her hand and then "unburned" it. She poured boiling water on her hand. She lay on the couch and tried to undo mentally what had been done. It was difficult because of the pain but she kept trying. She redid the scene and poured the boiling water on the tea and brewed it and then she drank the tea.

She did it over and over and finally in the act of thus making the tea she fell asleep. When she awoke some hours later there was no trace of the burn. She wrote: "You would have thought I should go right to the hospital, but now there is not even a sign of the burn."

The past and present are one in a greater moment.

CHAPTER 9

THE MYSTERY CALLED CHRIST

Among Blake's letters, there is one he wrote to the Reverend Dr. Trusler, who had criticized him, and said to Blake, "You need someone to elucidate your works."

So, Blake responded by saying, "You ought to know that what can be made explicit to the idiot is not worth my care. And the wisest of the Ancients considered what was not too explicit the fittest for instruction, because it rouses the faculties to act."

Then he went on to say to this Reverend, "Why is the Bible more instructive and entertaining than any book in the world? Is it not because it is addressed to the Imagination, which is Spiritual Sensation, and only mediately to Understanding or Reason?"

Well, of course, the Reverend did not understand that. Like most religious teachers of the world, he treated it solely as secular history; and Blake knew from his own experience that it was not. It was God's plan of Salvation.

Man must experience Scripture for himself before he can begin to understand how altogether wonderful it is. It's altogether true, but not on this level. Eternity is actually within your Immortal Head; and that's where the entire drama unfolds.

Now, let us turn to this Book that Blake called "the greatest book in the world" – and I will endorse that. I haven't read all the books, but I do not know of anything that could come near the Bible in revelation. It hasn't a thing to do with science. It's not teaching us anything about the stars; about anything in politics; it is all about God's plan of Salvation.

Here we turn, now, to the very first book of the New Testament: Matthew. "This is the book of the genealogy of Jesus Christ, son of David, son of Abraham. Here it establishes the 3 important characters of Scripture.

Now, we go back to Genesis, and start with the first one: Abraham. "And the Lord tempted Abraham." "Tested" might make for a better translation. "And the Lord tested Abraham and said to him: Take your son – your only son – Isaac, and offer him as a burnt offering."

And Abraham took his son the very next day, with the fire and the wood and the knife, and two young men, and went up to Mt. Moriah. If you are familiar with the story, we need not tell you the entire thing, but that is the story.

The Lord intervened, Abraham having met the test. He said to him, "Do not lay your hand upon the lad, for you obeyed the voice of the Lord." And then he made him the "father of the multitudes," for the name "Abraham" means "father of the multitudes," and said to him, "They will be more numerous than the stars, more numerous than the sands of the beach."

Well, just estimate that number, beyond the wildest dreams of man. That will be his offspring, yet he only had one son.

Now we know that's a lie right away, if you take it historically, because twelve years before the birth of Isaac the Lord gave him a son whose name was Ishmael, born of a slave in the household of his wife Sarah, for she was barren and it was beyond – well, bearing. "It had ceased to be with her after the affairs of women," – after the nature of woman.

So, finding herself barren and wanting a son and an heir, she sent her servant Hagar in to her husband Abraham, that he may "know" her, which, as the story is told, he did, and she bore him a son, and the Lord said, "Call him Ishmael," which means "God hears" or "God has heard."

That's twelve years prior to the birth of Isaac. Yet we are told — and these are the words of the Lord, "Take your son, your only son, Isaac — and offer him as a burnt offering.

How can the one who gave him a son called Ishmael now call this one his only son? The word translated "son and only son" appears only twelve times in the Bible, for the word "one" is "yaw-khad." This is translated and defined as "one, the only one; the unique one; my darling, my chosen one" — any term of endearment. These are the definitions given to the word that is now translated "your son, your only son."

Now, here, we turn now to the 22d Psalm, which you find quoted all throughout the New Testament. It's the Psalm of David. It begins: "My God, my God, why hast Thou forsaken me?" This is the cry on the Cross. Yet, the words are the words of David.

We find the first verse, the 8th verse, the 18th verse, all through the New Testament; and all these are the words of David. We find the same correspondence between the sufferings of Christ and the sufferings of David. Identical words are used, and they are all, now, in David's words.

Now, in the 22d Psalm, David sings out to his father the cry of despair, and he said, "Defend me", or "Deliver me from the sword." "Deliver my soul from the sword, and my life from the power of the dog." Why "my life"?

That's the same word translated "your son, your only son"; so why do they now translate it "my life"? The Hebrew word is "yaw-khad," and it means, "your son, your only son. David is saying, "Deliver your son, your only son, from the power of the dog."

In the Second Psalm David has already declared, "The Lord said unto me, Thou art my son. Today I have begotten thee." Now he calls upon the Lord, who seemingly has abandoned him, when he said, "My God, my God, why hast Thou forsaken me?"

Now, "Deliver," - not my life, - "Deliver your son, your only son, from the power of the dog." Now we come into the New Testament and we find that all the things said of David are now said of Jesus Christ. What is the secret?

Imagine this with me. Can you imagine a command that is absolute - a thing to be done absolutely and continuously; something stated in the imperative passive mood, like this:

"Thy will must be being done. Thy kingdom must be being restored."

It's the imperative passive mood. Think of the simple occurrence of an action, without reference to completeness or incompleteness; without reference to duration or repetition; without reference, specifically, to its position in time, but sometimes with reference to past time.

Just imagine such an action taking place forever and forever, and there is no limit to its duration. No one knows when the Father will stop the action – when God, who set the command in force, will stop it. So, we do not know the measure of the time.

It has no reference to its position in time, whether it's the First Year BC, the First Year AD, or the year 1971. We do not know; there's no reference to position in time. So, think of such an action.

Now, you and I have to re-enact this eternal command. You and I will have the experience recorded in that 22d chapter of Psalms, when suddenly we are going to experience it, now, in the real way, for these are all adumbrations. The entire Old Testament is an adumbration – that is, a foreshadowing in a not-altogether conclusive or immediately evident way.

It's a sketchy representation, omitting details, omitting all the little things that you could add into it and put into it and see the picture. It's a very, very sketchy picture.

Now we are coming to the story of David and it takes on more form now. "Say unto my servant David, When you lie down with your fathers," - which is a euphemism for "death," – when you die and sleep with your fathers, "I will raise up your son after you, who shall come forth from your body. I will be his Father, and he shall be my son."

That adumbration is taking on more fleshly states now. It's coming down to the story of Jesus Christ, who is coming out of David. Well, now, who is David? David is the symbol of humanity. Abraham is the symbol of the Father of Eternity, "the father of the multitudes." Who could that be, other than God?

So, here we have Abraham – the symbol of the Father, David – the symbol of humanity; and at the end of the journey something comes out of humanity which is the Son of God that is God. So, in the New Testament, the Son is made to say:

"I and my Father are one."

"He who sees me has seen the Father."

Yet, "The Father is greater than I."

He is telling us that I am not inferior to my Essential Being, the Father; only in my present capacity or office as the "sent," called the Son, am I inferior, but not as to my Essential Being, the Father.

When I am "sent," it's the Father who's sent. The Father sent me. Well, He had no one else to send but Himself; so He sent me. In the capacity – in the office of the "sent" - I seem inferior to my Self, the "Sender," but the "Sender" and the "sent" are one. That's what we are told in Scripture.

"He who sees me sees Him who sent me." So, if you knew my Father, you know Me; and if you know Me, you know my Father, for we are one. "I and my Father are one."

So, here we find Abraham only the symbol of God the Father, David the symbol of humanity, and Jesus Christ the symbol of the Son of God which is one with God. "I and my Father are one."

So, out of humanity God plays all the parts, may I tell you? There is not one part in the world that God isn't playing. And having played all the parts, He extracts from the experiences of humanity that which represents, now, the Son; and that Son is called "David," for David is the symbol of humanity.

Do you understand what Blake meant when he said it's the most entertaining book in the world, and not one book in the world compares to it? It's the most instructive book and the most entertaining book. It's like quicksilver. You are just about to grasp the Son, and he turns into the Father.

You are about to grasp the feeling of the Father, and He turns into the Son, just like quicksilver. He simply loses Himself and eludes your grasp in His many metamorphoses. Suddenly He is not the Father; He is the Son. So, now, "I say to you," said he at the very end of the story, "as the Father sent me, so send I you."

He's playing the part, now, of the Father. He's no longer, now, the Son; He has departed the world, and has returned to Himself the Father. "I will leave the world and go unto the Father." "I came out from the Father and came into the world. Again, I am leaving the world and going to the Father."

So, I return to my Self, who sent Himself as me; so He comes into the world as the Son, and while he's in the world as the Son, having the experiences of humanity, he seems inferior to Himself the Father, and He is, for He took upon Himself the restrictions and the limitations of humanity.

Now we are told, when he went towards the Cross, he carried his own wooden cross on his back. Now, Abraham placed upon Isaac the wood upon his back. Isaac wondered, Where is the lamb for the sacrifice? for he sees now the wood and he is carrying it on his back. His father has the knife to slay him and he has the fire to burn that wood. He is going to burn him.

"Burning" is the experiences of man. Don't think you haven't been burned! I don't mean in flames. The experiences are the burnings that you have in this world. It's from innocence through experience back to God the Father as an Awakened Imagination. That's the whole story.

So, here, the father said to him, "God Himself will supply the lamb." He is the lamb – the symbol of the lamb.

Let's go back now to the 22d chapter of the Book of Psalms. Remember what we told you in the 22d chapter of the Book of Genesis.

He took two young men, and he took his son, his only son. Here now, the cry of David, "Deliver me," - your son, your only son – "from the power of the dog." Now you read that, and you wonder, What on earth are they talking about? I have many Bibles at home. I haven't found one Bible that comes near the experience because they are writing and speculating.

They are theorizing; they have not had the experience. But the day that you meet David, who reveals you as God the Father, is the most exciting moment in Eternity. And there are two young men, and they stand – You are "in spirit," but you are all-wise at that moment. David is obvious, the most beautiful lad you could put your eyes on, a lad in his teens – early teens, beautiful beyond description.

He symbolizes humanity. You have passed through all that man could ever put upon you. You have borne the burden the allotted time, and now they are going to restore your long-lost rank. You were God before you came down, and you are going to be God by going back, but you will be enhanced by reason of the experience of becoming man.

So, you are looking at David. And here, to your right, are the two young men. In the Bible, for reasons which might be obvious, they are spoken of as "dogs." Look up the word "dog" in the Biblical Concordance, and you will see it means a "male harlot," – homosexuals in the service of the priest in the temple. That's who they were.

But this story was "before that the world was." It didn't develop. They were part of God's plan in the beginning of time; so here they are. You do not hurt them. You are the Father now, the father of David who symbolizes humanity.

You are looking at this beautiful creature, and they are looking at him, too. You are looking at him as a father to a son, "eating" him for his joy, his beauty, all that he means to you, his love; he is your darling, as the word also means "my darling."

But they are looking at him lustfully; they are looking at him in the most lustful manner and you warn them of his victory. He has never failed because the Lord was with him. The day the Lord anointed him "the spirit of the Lord came upon him mightily from that day forward, and never left David." So, David never lost a battle.

Here is the head of the giant before you – this enormous head, severed from the body as David severed the head from the body. And there it is on a table right before you, and here are these two. You don't do a thing about it; it's part of the "play."

This "play" has been taking place "before that the world was"; and no one knows when it is going to come to an end. I can't conceive of it coming to an end until every one of us experiences the play and becomes the father of David, for it is simply God returning to Himself. That's the story.

God came out from Himself into the world, penetrated these bodies, annexed these brains of ours, and made them a portion of Himself – a temporary portion. So, while He "wears" the body, the body is a part of the soul of the one who wears it. He will take it off – just drop it; it means nothing. But while he wears it in this world, it is a part of the soul of the one who wears it.

So, here, the "garment" is not the man. The garment is simply just what it is. It is a garment of flesh and blood "worn" while he is in the world of the experience of man.

But I tell you from experience, you won't have to wait a second when you take off that "garment" to see what it really is – as opposed to what you thought it was. And when they are crying and weeping because you took it off, you can't believe that they could be so silly, but you were equally silly before you took it off. But nevertheless, you see it.

Before I came out tonight, this University student from UCLA – he sits with my wife while I come to the lectures because we need someone to answer the phone and to be present; and before my friend arrived to bring me here, we got to talking about these things – these matters. He is from Cairo; he's an Egyptian. And he said to me, "You know, my father had this dream.

He dreamt that a friend of his was walking down the street with him; and as they were walking down the street, the friend fell, and there he died. He was dead, and many of the people came around and they began to cry and to weep.

They were all looking at him, and they were weeping. A week later he dropped dead; and the identical thing my father saw – he actually saw him saying to my father, 'What are they crying about?'"

Here was the garment; they were crying over the garment that he had taken off. I have seen it time and time again. So, I cannot be disturbed when a man takes off his "garment." Yes, you miss the contact – the little physical contact; but the Being who "wore" it is now clothed again in a garment just like it, but young – altogether young and healthy.

Whatever was missing before is not missing now. He is returned and restored to a healthy youth – not a baby, - young, - I would say about twenty. If he died at a hundred, he's now twenty; and he goes through the same world of man – the same terrestrial world – to have the experiences that he must have in order to confront David.

These are the three characters, each as a symbol: Abraham the symbol of God the Father, David the symbol of humanity, and Jesus Christ the symbol of

God the Father having gone through the experiences, because David, now, in the spirit, calls him, "Father."

"What think ye of the Christ?" he asked. They said, "The son of David."

He said, "Well, how then in the spirit did David call him, My Lord?" If David calls him, "My lord," how can he be David's son?

So, he's telling you that David belongs here. It's the sum total of all the experiences of humanity; and it's a beautiful experience when the whole thing is over.

Here it seems such a horrible thing, but when it's all over the result is transcendent, - but that which comes out as the one who was "sent" to have the experience, because the Father sent Himself as the Son, and Jesus Christ is the one having the experience.

It is Christ-in-you that is the hope of glory. Were he not in you, you could not have the experience of being man; and so he suffers, and you call it that you are suffering. But as Blake said it so beautifully:

"Babel mocks, saying there is no God nor Son of God: that Thou, O Human Imagination, o Divine Body... art all a delusion; but I know Thee, O Lord, when Thou arisest upon My weary eyes, even in this dungeon and this iron mill... Thou also sufferest with me, although I behold Thee not."

You can't behold the Being that is having the experience as you do objects in space, because the Being having the experience is that which is called "Imagination." You can't behold imagination. Imagination is the reality that is called this-thing-called-God. So, the Voice answers, and it's your own wonderful human imagination answering:

Fear not! I am with you always. Only believe in me, that I have power to raise from the dead Your brother who sleeps in" – this world called – "Albion."

Every one will rise. Not one can stop – they couldn't even stop it if they wanted to. There is no such thing as complete annihilation. There is no annihilation. You gave it up in the beginning to come here; and when you came here, you completely forgot – total amnesia; you forgot Who-You-Were. Listen to these words:

"Return unto me the glory that was mine, the glory that I had with Thee before that the world was."

This is not new. You gave up the Fatherhood, and yourself came into the world as the Son – the one that is "sent," - the one that is now to be made a burnt offering. And you are the "burnt offering" in this world, and you pass through hell in this world; but you are still one with the Father!

"I and my Father are one," – even though "My Father is greater than I," for I'll return to my Self, the Father, having experienced what I came out to experience; and I as Father will be enhanced by the experience of being man.

So, every one is going to have it. Not one will fail.

So, today if I really see it clearly, you'll see this peculiar mystery in the Bible. The whole vast world is yourself "pushed out," and all these characters are simply states of consciousness into which you can in one little moment vanish. You try to grasp him, and all of a sudden, he vanishes into this one, into that one.

You can't quite put your hand upon Him. But you do, in the depths of your Being; and you bring back glimpses of it, and then you share it with your brothers, because in the end we are all one, and yet without loss of identity.

You'll be God the Father, the father of David. And I know I am God the Father, the father of David; and yet, we are the same father! We have the same son, and yet we have no loss of identity. That is something that is difficult to explain.

So, this comes to us – this mystery called "Christ". He comes to us as one unknown, but not from the outside. He is on the inside. He rises in us as "one unknown," in the most strange, wonderful, and ineffable way. He is That One who lets us experience Who-He-Is.

You don't see Him; you experience being Him, because He was called "Father" by David, and David is going to call you "father." And may I tell you? when he does, it's not a shock; it's only the returning of memory. You know that you have always been That that was taking place in the beginning of time; but no one could attain to that bliss, except he was generated on earth.

So, man had to come down, that is, God had to come down and be generated on earth and re-enact the drama that is eternal, for that drama was simply an adumbration. It was a sketchy representation, omitting all the details.

We came down here, and we go through the "furnaces"; and having the experiences here on earth while we walk as man, it becomes a cubic reality. And now we know the meaning of these sketches that we read in the Bible. We see, now, what the two young men were that Abraham took with him up to Mt. Moriah. He took two young men, and he took his son.

Well, here was my son, and he wasn't called "Isaac"; he was called "David," and here were two young men. It does not describe what they were in the Bible. I know what they are. I know they are men who looked lustfully at my darling – at my son; and I simply warned them of the past.

I warned them of what took place, because he won the battle against the giant; and he who wins that battle against the giant who would destroy Israel sets his own father free, for the promise is: "The man who brings down the enemy of Israel, I will set his father free."

So, here is the giant's head severed from the body. And who is the father of the one who brought him down? Well, I am. What is the father's name in the Bible? The father's name is Jesse. Do you know what the word "Jesse" means? "Jehovah exists." That's what it means. It is any form of the verb "to be," - in other words, the one who bears the name "I AM." But its true definition is "Jehovah exists."

And here, the father is looking at his son. Now you know Who- You-Are. When, in "The Marriage of Heaven and Hell", Blake wrote in a very cryptic manner:

After the death of Christ, he became Jehovah.

He returned to Himself – Jehovah. In the end, there is nothing but the Lord God, Jehovah. There's nothing but God!

So, He sends Himself into the world; and the thing "sent" is the Son. He comes bearing witness of his Father, and we speak of him in the Bible as "Jesus, the Lord" or "Jesus Christ." He is the Savior. Well, the only Savior in the Bible is Jehovah Himself, as told us in the 43d and the 45th chapters of the Book of Isaiah:

"I am the Lord your God, the Holy One of Israel, your Savior; and besides Me there is no Savior."

So, if He comes as Savior, He is Jehovah. And so, when He departs, He returns to Himself, the Lord God Jehovah. There is nothing but God in the world, in spite of all the horror. But this is the flame spoken of in Scripture. These are the burns.

"Father, I see the knife, I see the wood. I am carrying the wood. I see the flame...but where is the lamb?"

See the imagery of the lamb, the symbol of the lamb? And in the end, the Father Himself really plays the part; but in playing the part, He appeared as the Son, because there is only God the Father.

So, every one is going to have the experience of Scripture, and I can't tell any one what a thrill it is when it begins to unfold within you. It comes so suddenly, without warning, and suddenly – all within your head. That's why I started off by telling you Eternity dwells within your Immortal Head.

That is an immortal head. The whole "play" is taking place there; but in the fullness of time you'll experience it. It is taking place. It is a command that must be done absolutely and continuously, without reference to position in time, without any reference as to its completeness or incompleteness; but it is not completed until man-on-earth replays the drama.

And he does it – when he re- plays it within himself, it takes on the cubic reality, while as it is told through the medium of the Prophets, it is a sketchy representation, omitting all the details. That's why the one who wrote the Epistle to the Hebrews could say that "in many and various ways God spoke of old to our fathers by the prophets, but in these last days He has spoken to us by a son."

There's no further revelation than when the Son appears, for then you know Who-You-Are. And what man is seeking in this world is the Father. Every one is seeking the Father, the Cause of the phenomena of life. There's only one Cause; and blessed is the man who is freed from the tyranny of second causes! So, there is only one Cause, and that is God the Father.

So, as God the Father tempted Abraham, He was tempting Himself, for he's only the symbol of Himself. Can I really go through hell and return? Can I die, and rise? And God took the challenge. He could die and rise! But in rising, He enhanced the brilliance of Himself the greatness of Himself, because there is no limit to expansion, no limit to His wonderful transcendency.

He placed the limit upon opacity and upon contraction; and that limit is man. So, when He became man − and He could not play that He is man − He isn't pretending that He's man, - He is man. He becomes man! Even though it's a temporary "garment" that He wears, while He "wears" it, He is so identified with it, He feels that "It's myself." You cut Him, and He hurts.

You chop off a finger and He says, "I've lost my finger." He is so much a part of the "garment" that He "wears" that He can't separate Himself from it, seemingly. But the day will come, He will simply take it off and return to Himself, but He will be enhanced by reason of the experience in this journey as man.

But when the day comes for the individual, no one knows of that hour, of that day; only the Father knows. No one knows but the Father. Let no one tell you that they can tell you when it's going to happen. I know from my own experience it comes so suddenly.

Little did I expect the night I went to bed in San Francisco that that night, on July the 20th, 1959, was the night. Nor on the 6th day of December of the same year, did I know that that night the Fatherhood of God would be revealed to me by His Son, who would call me "father."

Little did I know of the Ascent into Heaven on the morning of the 8th of April of the following year, 1960; and then January the 1st, 1963, when the dove descended in bodily form and smothered me with kisses, which was the Descent of the Holy Spirit in the form of a dove.

Therefore, that was the climax of it all. That was putting the seal of approval on the journey; and you simply, now, delay your departure to tell and encourage those who are ready to hear it.

So, those who are ready to hear it are hearing it. And you can then spread the word, and tell it. You will tell it first as hearsay; but eventually you will tell it from experience, for the Evangelists in writing the story in our Gospels – they simply related their own experience. They were not telling it from hearsay.

They told exactly what happened to them, but they told it for reasons known to them in the third person. So they spoke of "him" constantly, but they are really telling their own experience. But no one in my spirit world has curtailed my tongue; so I was not commanded to tell it in the third person. I was simply told to tell it, and so I tell it as I must tell it, in the first person, for I am telling and relating my own experience.

Everything spoken of in Scripture concerning the Lord Jesus Christ I have experienced. But I am limited while I "wear" this "garment" with all the weaknesses of the "garment," I have assumed it – all the limitations of the "garment" of flesh and blood, I have assumed it, and must continue to assume it until that moment in time when I take it off, and take it off for the last time.

Yet, I am one with those who have not yet taken it off, because there's only one Father. So, I cannot crow – I cannot raise my voice and simply yell, "I did it," although the 22d Psalm does end on a note of that nature: Posterity will sing His praises, and they will all say the Lord has wrought it.

All the things – the horrors of that 22d Psalm, beginning with the cry, "My God, my God, why hast Thou forsaken me?" and all the pleas that he makes to be delivered from all the things round about him; but in the end, the Lord wrought it, and unborn tomorrows will hear that it was done – it was accomplished; and that will encourage them to go on through the "furnaces of affliction."

"But how long, how vast, how severe" these furnaces before man actually discovers himself as God the Father "were long to tell."

But he will discover it, and he will know he is God the Father; for there is only God. Meanwhile, you take what I've told you so far concerning the Law, and apply it. Apply the Law. Your dreams, may I tell you? are most encouraging – most encouraging.

One who saw her husband encased in all kinds of limitations from the hips down, and before her eyes they all began to crack and break and fall apart, and then he jumped and danced for joy. So, take it just as you saw it. He is released; he has been freed from the restrictions, whatever they were, in the immediate present – completely freed. And many of you have these wonderful experiences.

Another one who sits next to her tonight, she had the dream of a wedding, and I was the only one –

seemingly – that they would discuss. I sat to her right at a very long table, but across the table; and they all wondered why Neville is here, because this was a Jewish wedding. And yet, she knew that I was going to give the main speech of the evening. "Why is he here?"

And so, I spoke in my own tongue, but each man heard me in his own tongue wherein he was born. And those who thought, because they were all Jewish, that they would not accept me – all but one accepted me. The one who was controversial in the beginning – he didn't understand one word that I said, but all the others that he thought would not accept me – well, I thought that was the most marvelous vision that she had.

And many of them, one after the other, - one has had one. I will tell you now concerning her and her husband: in her dream, she saw a snake – a rattlesnake, and the husband said, "I must take off the rattlers first"; so he began to take off the rattlers, and she handed him a hammer to beat it and to beat the snake to kill it. And in beating it, she awoke. Now, that is a different kind of a dream. That's a symbol of sex.

You cannot crush out sex on this level. It has to be something entirely different. You don't crush it out. You start to crush it out, and strange, peculiar dreams will possess you. It has to be transcended in the most normal, natural manner. It's not really transcended until you ascend into Heaven. That comes when your body is split from top to bottom, and you – like a fiery serpent – ascend into Heaven.

When you see that golden, liquid light at the base of your spine, after your body is severed in two from top to bottom, and you see that pool of golden, living, liquid light, and you fuse with it and you become it, and like a fiery serpent, up you go into Heaven, and you take it by force. You take it violently.

Now the energies that went down into generation are now reversed up into regeneration. But while they are still down, if you try to kill it, as many people do, from the early church members of the Catholic Church, – his name was Origen. He had himself castrated, that he would not be tempted by the women that he was teaching.

He was one of the true early fathers of the church. He was born – or, rather, he died – one hundred years before Augustine was born. That's how early he was. He came in the Second Century AD; and he was one of the moving spirits in the formation of the early church which was the Catholic Church. And you read the story in the Encyclopedia Britannica.

His name was Origen, and he castrated himself that he may not be disturbed when he had to face women and teach them the mystery of Christ. But he still could not cut it out that way. You can castrate the man, or woman, but it will still be in his imagination; and his dreams will still be of that nature. So, you cannot hit it and kill it.

It's simply something that leaves you by a reversal of energies. It turns from generation into regeneration.

CHAPTER 10

WHO IS THE REAL
MESSIAH?

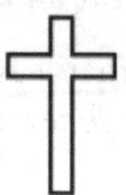

I t is in us as persons that God is revealed. "He who began a good work in you will bring it to completion at the day of Jesus Christ" [Philippians 1:6]. To say "Jesus Christ" is the same as saying "Jehovah's Messiah." Christ is Messiah.

This will not shock you because you have been coming – maybe all of you – for quite a while. It certainly would be a shock to the outer world to learn who Messiah is. But I am telling you from my own personal experience who He is.

We are told in Scripture, "He is the Son of God," [Acts 9:20]. I am telling you tonight who the Son of God really is; and you will never in Eternity find another Son – not in Eternity!

You and I were taught as Christians that Jesus Christ differs – is something entirely different from that of the Old Testament. Yet he is made to say, "I have come to fulfill Scripture," [Matthew 5:17]. "Scripture must be fulfilled in me,"[Luke 22:37].

"Then beginning with Moses and the law and the prophets and the Psalms, he interpreted to them in all the Scriptures the things concerning himself," [Luke 24:27].

He came only to do the Will of God. Now, in the 40th Psalm we are told: "I delight to do Thy will, O God. Thy law is within my heart." [Psalm 40:8]

This is the Psalm of David. It's the 40th Psalm. "I delight to do Thy will, O God." In the 13th Chapter of the Book of Acts, by the same author that gave us the Book of Luke, we are told – and this is the Lord speaking:

"I have found in David, the son of Jesse, a man after my own heart who will do all my will," [Acts 13:22] confirming the 40th Psalm, which is the Psalm of David: "I delight to do Thy will."

Well, I am telling you from my own experience, the day is coming – and I hope it's in the immediate present – that you will be set free. You'll be set free only as you find David. "If the Son sets you free, you are free indeed," [John 8:36]. Well, who are you? You are God the Father. That's who You are.

You came down and became man; but before you came down and became man, you had prepared a way for your Self to return, and only your "son," which is the result of your experiences in manhood – the result is David; and when you see the result of your experiences, and know then – like memory returning – who You are – you are set free as told us in the Book of Samuel.

He has promised to set the father of the one destroying the enemy of Israel – to set that father free. So he inquired. But who inquired? The king. But the king was insane; his name was Saul. He couldn't even remember that he met the lad and met the father of the lad prior.

Here in the 16th Chapter, he has asked the father of the lad to let the lad serve him. In the 17th Chapter he is inquiring: "Whose son are you, young man?"

"Inquire whose son – whose lad – the stripling is."

No one knows, because Saul is an insane man, as we are! You are not confined in some institution; but if you have lost your memory as to who You are, you are insane. You are suffering from amnesia. And in this case, although we are not violent, we are suffering from total amnesia, because we do not know our only "son."

That only son is David, named in the New Testament as Jesus Christ, which is Jehovah's Messiah. And David is the Messiah. "Rise and anoint him, for this is he, and then the spirit of the Lord came mightily upon David from that moment forward," [I Samuel 16:12-13]. He never lost a battle, because the Spirit of the Lord was with him. But to find David, what else is worthwhile in this world?

Maybe tonight you could use – and who could not – a fortune? Any one of us tonight could use an extra sum of money, no matter what it is. If I had tonight millions, I could still use another few. If you had only a few thousand, you could use a few thousand more. Every one can use it. But what is that, compared to the finding of the Son? "If the Son sets you free, you are free indeed," as told you in the 8th Chapter of John.

If the Son – and man is looking for the Son, and he is complacent – he is satisfied, because he has been taught to believe one called "Jesus Christ," born two thousand years ago is the Son. He has completely accepted that; he believes that, and he thinks that is going to set him free. It will not in Eternity set you free.

You must find, in the spirit, David; and David, in this spirit, is going to call you" Father." And when he calls you "Father," your whole memory returns. And that is God awakening!

You rise from the grave first, and still you do not know the Son. You are born from above, "not of blood nor of the will of the flesh nor of the will of man, but of God," [John 1:13] – born of your Self. You came out all by yourself. Yet, you are not free – not until you find the Son. And when you find him, it's told you in the form of a parable.

"For this your brother was dead, and is alive; he was lost, and he is found." [Luke 15:32]

And the one who complained never left home. He remained in the land of Innocence; he never entered the world of Experience. You entered the world of Experience; and having gone through all the fires of this world, you come out as God the Father.

To be a father, there must be a son; and the son, may I tell you? Is David. I will state it a thousand times over: there is no other son. "God and His Son" is the drama in this world.

You – sound asleep and completely oblivious as to who You are, suffering from total amnesia – only one thing in this world can ever bring back to you your memory, and that is the discovery of David. And when you find him, suddenly memory returns, and the whole thing unfolds within you. And you are the One who conceived the play, and did not pretend that you are man.

You actually became as we are, that we may be as You Are. So you became man that man may become God! but prepared the way for your return to your own Godhood.

Now we are told, "Be ye perfect, as your Father in Heaven is perfect," [Matthew 5:48]. The word "perfect" is "telos," which means "the end." It comes at the climax. It means to reproduce faithfully the original.

Well, God is the original. He comes down into this world, and in man reproduces faithfully Himself in man. And then He awakes having reproduced it, so that His Son "in the beginning" recognizes it, and brings back into His Eternal Being all of us.

So every one will awake. I can't conceive of failure. I can't conceive of one being in this world failing, because God the Father is in Him! Even if he dies as a little child, he once breathed. That breath was God.

"Nothing is impossible to God," [Luke 1:37]. The most horrible beast that walked the face of this earth in the form of man cannot fail to awake! I do not care what he is. Every being in this world, male and female, will awaken; and when they awaken, it's because the Son appears.

"No one knows who the Son is except the Father, and no one knows who the Father is except the Son and any one to whom the Son chooses to reveal it." [Matthew 11:27 and Luke 10:22]

So in the fullness of time, He sends His Son into our hearts crying "Father." And then, in that moment in time, the Son appears. He was always within us.

The whole vast thing takes place within the Immortal Head of man.

So when you depart, having found the Son, you will be part of the watchers, watching every one in the world; and they are all your brothers. And you will know that:

"What seems to be, Is, to those to whom It seems to be, and is productive of the most dreadful consequences to those to whom it seems to be, even of torments, despair, eternal death; but the Divine Mercy steps in and redeems Man in the one body called Jesus." [William Blake, from Jerusalem]

And "Jesus" is "Jehovah." "Jesus" is the word that means "Jehovah." "Christ" is "Messiah," the Son. So "Jesus Christ" is simply "Jehovah's Messiah." That Messiah is David. Jesus is the Lord God Jehovah.

His Son – if he is a father, he has a son, and the Son is David. There is no other Son.

"So David in the spirit calls Him "My Father" [Matthew 22:43] – my rock – "the Rock of my Salvation" [Psalm 89:26] – he calls Him "my God." So Jesus is the man that is "born from above," and the man "born from above" is Jehovah. He is God the Father; and if he is a father, there must be a son.

"Where is my son?" Then the Son comes, and he's David; and David brings back your memory, and you are set free. For: "If the Son sets you free, you are free indeed." This is the great mystery of the Christian faith. It's a mystery, not to be kept secret, but it is mysterious in character.

Scholarship is not enough to grasp the mystery of Scripture. In fact, when Paul sets out the eighth rank in the Kingdom of Heaven, he puts the wise, wise men at the bottom. People completely misunderstand what it means to be one who speaks in many tongues. That's the scholar.

It hasn't a thing to do with all this nonsense where people throw themselves into a trance, and then utter – bringing saliva into their mouth; it hasn't a thing to do with that. He mentions eight divisions, and you read it in the 12th Chapter of First Corinthians [I Corinthians 12:8-10].

The first is the apostle: that's always the first. Then the prophet; then the teacher; then the miracle worker; then the healer; then the helper; then the administrator; and then those who speak in diverse tongues, the scholar who will take our scripts and, year after year they will bring them back into their original position, because men invariably interfere with them.

More so in the past then today, because today we have print; and we can set a type and reproduce a thing over and over. But in the past, until the middle maybe of the Fifteen Century, everything was script; everything was copied.

Well, a man couldn't take these volumes and copy them accurately; so he not only miscopied, but he also inserted his own opinion. So the scholars who understood the vast background of language could take them and bring them back to their seeming original form. Yet they are the last in the ranks in Heaven.

The first is the Apostle. Well, who is the Apostle? The one who is called and sent. That's the Apostle. You are called into the presence of the Risen Lord. You answer the questions He asks you, which is the highest of all; it's above all the ranks, for Love is the greatest of all.

You could be the Apostle, you could be the Prophet; you could be any of these mentioned in the eight ranks, just as we have in Government. You come down from the head to the very lowest. In the Army, we start with the General down to the Private. We have it in the social world. But above all these ranks stands Love.

And so, every one, one day, will be embraced by "the One Body, the One Spirit. The One Lord. The one God and Father of all," and that Being is Love. So all will be equal, in spite of the parts we play in the world. So let no one "pull his rank" on you.

So he has been sent? Well, that's all right; he is sent, and maybe he is a Prophet, and maybe he is a healer, and maybe he can work miracles; but let no one "pull any rank" on you, because eventually you are going to be part of the Body of God, and Body's Immortal Body is LOVE.

All will then be members of the Body of God: "the one body, the one spirit, the one lord; one God and Father of all." So let no one "pull his rank" on you.

I have been called, and I have been sent. I am an Apostle. I stood in the presence of the Risen Lord, and He asked me to name the greatest thing in the world, and I answered in the words of Paul: "Faith, hope and love, these three; but the greatest of these is Love." [I Corinthians 13:15]

At that, he embraced me, and our bodies fused and we became one body without loss of identity. I was not absorbed into some world soul. I was one with that body of Love, one with that spirit, one with that God and Father of all – but no loss of identity.

Then I was "sent." To be "called" is to be "sent." But it was the embrace of Love that was the important thing, for that is above all ranks in the world.

So here, the day is coming – and I do hope it's soon for every one here – when you will find the Son; and when you find him, he is David – David of Biblical fame, the David mentioned in the Book of Samuel and the Book of Chronicles, the David of the Psalms; that is the David of whom I speak – the one who could say:

"I will tell of the decree of the Lord: He said unto me, 'Thou are my son, today I have begotten thee." [Psalm 2:7]

This is the David of whom I speak, and he is the Son of God; and Jesus Christ – Jesus is Jehovah, and "Christ" means "Messiah." That is the "Anointed One." And who was anointed? Was it not David?

"Rise and anoint him. That is he. And from that moment forward, the Spirit of the Lord descended upon him and possessed him;" and he lost not a battle, for the Spirit of God went with him.

So this is our destiny. You and I are destined to awaken as the Being that we really are. Now the word called "perfect" is "telos." It simply means the "end," the "climax;" it always comes at the end. And you will be saying these words, "I have finished the work Thou gavest me to do.

Now return unto me the glory that was mine, the glory that I had with Thee before that the world was," [John 17:4,5]. That's what you will say! You are only asking for the return of what you gave up to come down into the world of "death."

"I have finished the work," – that is what the word "telos" means: to finish it, to accomplish it; "and having finished it, I am only asking for the return of what was mine before that the world was." And "glory" means God Himself.

"Glorify Thou me with Thine own Self, with that glory which I had with Thee before that the world was." So what on earth could any one ask for that would be comparable to the discovery of the Son which brings his memory back? Well we are all suffering from amnesia.

If I could only remember that I am the Father! And there, as father, there is a son – and find the son that could I some way call me and then bring back my memory. And he does! He calls you, and your memory returns; and here you stand before your own "son" – your only "son," and then you know exactly who You are.

And you know how you did it! "Before that the world was," you prepared the way for your Self to return. And he – your "son" – did everything that you willed him to do. And now you would not leave his soul in hell. You redeem him, and you bring him back. And you and your "son" return.

Now the "son" is the sum total of all the experiences of humanity, fused into a single whole and projected – personified, and it comes out as David. And that is David. You cannot blame any one for not completely accepting the false concepts that we have given to the world as we teach Scripture.

Those who are grounded in the Old Testament, you can't blame them for not – unless they have the experience. When they have the experience, they will not go along with the traditional Christian concept; they will see their own wonderful state unfolding: that the Old Testament actually is true – it unfolds. And it is true in the New, but not as taught by those who teach it.

They teach it entirely differently. It's not so at all. God is the only Reality. There is nothing but God. And God is Love, and God is the Father; and as a father, there must be a child, and that child happens to be a son, and that "son" happens to be David. So I am telling you what I know from my own experience. I am not speculating; I am not theorizing.

If today we go back two thousand years, we think the most important people who lived in the First Century AD. would be the Caesars and the mighty powers of that day. They were the unknown fishermen. Name the others. The unknown fishermen of that Century were the most important.

So he comes into the world; and man, by his wisdom, did not know God. "So it pleased God by the foolishness that I preach" [See I Corinthians 1:21] said Paul, "to tell you of the mystery of God. And the weakness of man," – he uses that – "and the humbleness of man," – and he uses that – "and not all the false pride of the world."

Today we give awards to this one for being the best dressed. Well, she can afford a hundred thousand a year for dresses. The other one can afford another fortune for something else. And we give all these awards every year.

Ask me next year who was mentioned this year. They fade just as shadows fade. But we go back two thousand years when the unknown fishermen were the most important people who walked the face of the earth.

And he called them, one by one; and as he called them one by one, he embraced them and sent them. No one can be sent unless he is first called; and when he is called, he is embraced. But who embraced them? While he was on earth? No.

After he departed this world. It's the Risen God that calls them. The Risen Lord calls them; and when you are called into this, may I tell you? The story is so altogether true: There is here the angelic being with a recording book. How on earth could that be seen by Daniel? But it is true.

Here is a book that tall – a book that wide; and here she stands – or rather, she is seated at a desk not unlike this, but it's a big one, and she is recording – the Recording Angel. And when you are called into this Divine Assembly, you stand at her side, and she looks at you.

She doesn't say one word to you; she just simply records your name. She checks you off. Then you are taken, in spirit, into the presence of the Risen Lord, the Ancient of Days – that's who he is – as described in Daniel. And he asks you the simple question: "What is the greatest thing in the world?"

And you answer automatically, as though you were divinely prompted: "Faith, hope, and love — these three: but the greatest of these is Love." Then he actually embraces you. He has hands, he has a face, he has a mouth — he asks you a question.

And here, he embraces you and you fuse as though you took a drop of water and dropped it into a bowl of water. It disappears in it without loss of identity. It becomes the bowl, and yet it is still individualized. I did not cease to be aware that I am the being that I thought myself to be; yet I felt the ecstasy of the union.

That was union. That was the true baptism of the Holy Spirit. And then I was placed in the presence of another, who was Infinite Power; and it was he who sent me. He is the same one who embraced me, for God is a protean Being. He assumes any form that suits the purpose of the moment. So when I was sent, Power sent me; when I was embraced, Love embraced me.

That is for Eternity, as told in the 8th of Romans: "Nothing in Eternity can separate us from the love of God" [Romans 8:39]. So not a thing that I will go through, having been sent, can separate me from that union with Love. But I was sent, not by Love; I was sent by Power.

He seemed to be Almighty Power when he sent me. "Down with the blue bloods," – not the social structure. Down with all external worship – it simply is an expression meaning all church protocol: everything that is something on the outside – down with it. It hasn't a thing to do with Reality.

All the things you see when you go to church – all the crosses and all the things – down with it! Do not tear it down – ignore it. It hasn't a thing to do with reality. So, Power sent me to tell you what I am telling you; but Love first embraced me, and therefore I am persuaded that not a thing in this world can separate me from the Love of God.

No matter what I go through, it can't separate me from the Love of God. But I am telling you, you are God the Father. You will not awake until the Son appears.

At that moment in time when he appears, your memory returns, and you recognize him in the most intimate, marvelous manner; and no power in the world can shake your confidence in this union of father & son.

It's the return of memory. Amnesia vanishes, and your Godhood returns. But you know every one is going to have the identical experience. You cannot boast, as you are told in First Corinthians, the 4th Chapter: "What have you that you did not receive? If you received it, where can you boast?" [I Corinthians 4:7]

Of what could you boast? How could I stand before you and boast that I was embraced by God when it was a gift? God gives to Himself! So I can't boast. I am not better than – if I precede you in a chronological order, I can't precede you in importance, because we are all one.

Every one is God! So if I preceded you – undoubtedly I have by a few years – it's twelve years this coming month that it happened to me. It could happen to you tonight. It may happen to you at the end of a section of time. But when it happens, you have been one with me.

I can't be better than – and time will mean nothing if I preceded you in time. It hasn't a thing to do with taking precedence over you, because we are one. God is one. So here, the whole unfolds within man – the skull of man, the Immortal Head of man. That's where the whole drama is.

If you dwell upon this, may I tell you? You will have such courage to face everything in this world. If business is slow, what does it matter? If someone that you love dearly is fading before your eyes – all right, you know, she or he is still the Being the you are. Nothing dies in this world. And so, it really doesn't matter.

If they fade and they disappear from your world, it still doesn't matter because you are love, and he or she is love; and all, in the end, are one. All are one. So you are encouraged to go through all the fires of the world – all the hell that one can put upon you, because we are all one, and we cannot come out until we are perfect. You must be perfect, as your Father in Heaven is perfect.

And that "perfect" means simply "fully made," "fully grown," a full man; and that full man is God. God is man. Let no one tell you that He is not. He is not some impersonal over-soul. God is man!

Man not knowing this on this level, he thinks He is some peculiar impersonal force. He is not an impersonal force; He is very personal. One body, one spirit. One lord, one God, and Father of all. All are contained within this "One."

So I ask you to be patient. And if you can't completely grasp all that I am trying to say, believe me. I am telling you what I know from my own personal experience. I am not speculating; I am not theorizing.

I have no intention whatsoever to set up some workable philosophy of life. I have no −ism, no desire to set anything in motion to perpetuate what I am talking about. If any one has that desire, let them have it; but I have one. I do know that it will last and last and last, and grow, just as it grew two thousand years ago.

For the time has come to tell you the truth concerning the Son. We have had it now for two thousand years − a misconception of who God really is. Jesus is the Lord God Jehovah. And the Lord God Jehovah is a father; and the Father has a Son, and that Son is David. That is the David of Biblical fame.

And one day you will know it, and you will be so thrilled, you can't conceive of the ecstasy that is yours when you see David, and David calls you "father!" And then you go back into your own words because you dictated the words of Scripture and fell asleep. You are the Author of the Book!

"In the volume of the book, it is all about me. I delight to do Thy will, O My Lord," [Psalm 40:7,8]. It's all about me: the Father and the Son. This is the relationship. And when it happens to you, you will tell it.

And I am – telling you from my own experience that unborn generations will take what you hear tonight and tell it and tell it and tell it. I mean unborn generations throughout the centuries, for I've been sent to tell it.

The year was 1929 when I was called. In 1929 I was called and sent, and I did not understand anything concerning the mystery that happened that night. But He takes the lowest of men, the humblest of men – not the scholars.

He takes those that no one would ever suspect; and if He takes you, well then, He is with you, and He unfolds Himself within you. So, in due time, thirty years later He unfolded Himself within me – in 1959. It took Him thirty years in preparation within me, like a gestation; and then suddenly He rose within me. Then I knew who He was.

He came to me as one unknown, yet one who in the most wonderful, miraculous manner allowed me to experience who He is. When I experience who He is, I realized I am He. There were not two of us then – just one. I was all alone in the tomb wherein I was buried, and I didn't realize throughout the years that I was the One spoken of in Scripture – that I was the buried one.

Now let me comfort you. "We have been crucified with Christ" – not just a single being – "we have been crucified with Christ. Nevertheless I live, yet not I, it is Christ who lives in me; and the life I now live, I live by the faith of that Son of God who loved me," – his Father "gave Himself for me" [Galatians 2:19,20].

He "died" to bring his Father back. This is part of the drama. The Father and the Son. Only God could do it! There is nothing but God in the world.

God is playing every part in the world; and in the end, when He awakes, his beloved David stands before him – the sum total of the Father's experiences through death. And he conquers death. He comes out of death, as the Immortal Being that he is.

Now if you know of anything in this world worthwhile more than what I have told you tonight, name it for me. If tonight you owned the earth, and death, may I tell you? Is inevitable, what would it matter what you owned? If you were the most famous person in the world, what would it matter if death terminates it?

I tell you that you are an Immortal Being, infinitely greater than any outside man in the world. No position could ever be given you comparable to the

Being that you really are. You are the Immortal God. You are God the Father.

If any one should doubt me tonight, I would not question you. You only know this much: I'll meet you in Eternity, and we will laugh at your doubt! I would not care if you doubted or not, we will meet in Eternity.

There will be no need for forgiveness, because we will simply be hilarious that in your present state of consciousness you could doubt that you are the Being I am telling you that you are. Having awakened from the dream of life, I am telling you who You are. And so, should you doubt it, I will only have to wait; and I will wait patiently and then embrace you lovingly as my brother, for we are all brothers.

It takes all the brothers to form God the Father. Every one is a Brother; and together, collectively, we form God the Father. You see, the word "Elohim" is a plural word. It's a compound unity: one made up of others. We are the "others." We are the Brothers.

So, "In the beginning God" – that word is "Elohim" a plural word –"said, 'Let us make man in our image.'"

That is a plural word, and the word is Elohim." So we are the ones who make it in our image. It must be faithfully reproduced. What? The original. We are the original. It must be faithfully reproduced to expand the glory that is ours!

When it is faithfully reproduced, then it is perfect, when you awake; but you have expanded by reason of the experience of coming into the world of "death." Now, if this is not practical tonight, may I tell you? It's far more practical than anything that you would ever hear in the world.

In the morning's paper you read of prominent men. It's always prominent if it is in the theatrical world and big, or if it has money. It doesn't ask you how you got the money; but you could leave, say, fifty million tonight, even though you stole the fifty million, and you are going to get a long, long obituary tomorrow; but you aren't going to take it with you.

You will leave your fifty whatever-it-is for others to either spend or invest as they do; but they aren't going to take it with them. I ask you to live nobly, because now you know who You are. Live so that you mind can store a past worthy of recall. Well, you are simply going to leave the little things behind you, but you will take over your past.

I will know – you will know – when you go beyond. In my own case, I am not going beyond. I have finished the race. I can actually say with Paul: "I have fought the good fight. I have finished the race. I have kept the faith. Henceforth is laid up for me the Crown of Righteousness" [II Timothy 4].

So, I am not continuing the race, continuing the fight; I will only continue it for a little while, to get off all that I am told I must get off before the curtain comes down, which in my own case – without being sad about it – I personally hope it isn't too long. Personally, I hope it's not beyond the immediate present.

That is my personal hope. But I do know we all come in on time, and we go out on time. So I cannot tell anyone because no one knows that hour, that moment, but the Deep, and He doesn't reveal it to the surface mind. He simply reveals it at that moment when you go.

But I as a being still living on the surface for a little while –it would be my wish that it would not be long delayed, because I have finished it. I have done all that I am called upon to do. "I have finished the work Thou gavest me to do. Now return unto me the glory that was mine, the glory that I had with Thee before that the world was." That is my prayer tonight.

I do hope that you will be encouraged, no matter what happens to you in the present or the future, to remember these words that you really are God the Father. If you are beaten down and you are ostracized and you are alone, remember: You are God the Father!

And remember my words: You are going to find your "son" who is God's Son, and God's Son is going to call you "Father," and you will know you really are God the Father! And whatever clothes you have worn – how tattered they might have been in the world, when you hear it, you will be clothed in your Immortal Body.

CHAPTER 11

CHRIST IN YOU

"Examine yourselves to see if you are holding to your faith. Test yourselves! Do you not realize that Jesus Christ is in you?" Now, faith is not complete until through experiment it becomes experience!

When you test the Christ in you and prove from experience that it works, then you have the faith. But first you must find who Christ is, where he is, and what he is. You are not called upon to test a tradition of man as something on the outside, but Jesus Christ who is in you!

Perhaps you heard on the news tonight that the Catholics have just eliminated forty saints. For hundreds of years millions of people have prayed to

Saint Christopher, yet now they are being told that he never existed. How many St. Christopher medals and figurines were sold to protect those who went into battle or traveled afar?

Believing he was the saint of the traveler, how many put their faith in him? Santa Barbara was named after Saint Barb, who is now believed to be non-existent, yet the cause of the recent broken oil line!

If you will read scripture carefully (and not go along with the herd) you will see that there is no intermediary between yourself and God. No priest or saint, minister, truth teacher, or so-called healer can be an intermediary between you and God. Christ in you is your hope of glory.

You must examine yourself to see if you are holding to this faith. Test yourself. Do you not realize that Jesus Christ is in you? If you do, put him to the test. He is your power to create, your power to imagine everything – be it good, bad, or indifferent.

The 14th chapter of the Book of John begins: "Let not your hearts be troubled." This statement is repeated in different ways over and over again by the master of souls – who is Christ in you, for when he awakens fear is abolished.

Awake, he urges you to fear not, be not afraid, be not troubled. A tyrant could not exist without fear.

He must scare us to death before he can rule us. By slaughtering millions (and you are afraid you will be next) he has you under his power.

But if you know you and your family cannot die, you will not be afraid and there would be no tyrant. Tyranny can exist only in a frightened world. So, Awakened Imagination begins the 14th chapter of John by saying: "Let not your heart be troubled, you believe in God, believe also in me.

In my Father's house are many mansions. If it were not so would I have told you that I go to prepare a place for you? And when I go and prepare a place for you, I will come again and take you to myself, that where I am there you may be also. Now the place you know and the way you know."

Then Thomas said, 'Lord, we do not know where you are going, so how can we know the way?' and he replied, 'I am the way and the truth and the life.' Then Philip said, 'Show us the Father and we will be satisfied.' And he answered, 'I have been so long with you and yet you do not know me Philip? He who has seen me has seen the Father. How then can you say, 'Show us the Father?'"

Let us take this verse on this level first and then take it into the higher level. In my Father's house are many mansions. The word translated "mansion" means to stay in a certain place; state; relation; or expectancy."

There are infinite states from which you may view the world. You may enter a state and abide there until it becomes your home or you could be simply passing through for a moment, but it is a state, one of your Father's mansions.

Choose the mansion in your Father's house that you would like to enter. Assume you are already there. Feel the reality of the state surround you and you have arrived. Your dream is now true, but you must abide there! When you leave tonight you expect to return to the place you left to come here. At the moment this auditorium is solid and real, while your home is only a mental image. So what is a home? It is the state to which your thoughts most constantly return.

Are you thinking from the state you desire? Or is your dream just a passing fancy, a daydream you enjoyed for the moment and then dropped? You can tell if you abide in your house of desire by watching your thoughts, for the state in which you most constantly return constitutes your dwelling place.

When you imagined you were the person you wanted to be and heard your friends rejoice at your good fortune, you entered that state and prepared a place in which to dwell; for at that moment Christ in you was speaking to the outer, rational you.

As your own wonderful human imagination Christ is telling you that he knows you are afraid, that you have obligations in life which must be met, but to not be afraid for "I will go and prepare a place for you." Knowing this, close your physical eyes upon the world round about you and let not your heart be troubled, neither let it be afraid, for all things are possible to Christ in you!

Let him prepare the state, for he is the way to its fulfillment. Closing your eyes against the facts of life, dare to assume you are seeing and hearing what you would see and hear if your desire were true. Now, tune it in as you would a radio. If, when you turned on the radio four or five stations are heard at the same time, you couldn't stand the confusion and would turn the radio off. So it is with your imagination – it must be fine-tuned.

Now no radio or TV is comparable to you, for that which the mind creates cannot be greater than the mind who created it. We are amazed at the perfection of a little instrument called a radio because it can produce sound out of the nowhere, yet the mind that is so amazed is the one who created it.

Our radio or television can be carried around the house or yard with no connection to a charge of electricity, yet the sound and picture come through perfect, and any station (or channel) can be reached by merely a flick of the wrist. At this moment everything that is being broadcast or telecast in the world is in this room, but we haven't tuned it in.

Now, you have an instrument infinitely greater than any radio or television, but it must be turned on and fine tuned. Think of a friend who would truly rejoice in your good fortune. Tune him in until his is the only voice you can hear. Let him tell you of his thrill because of your good fortune.

Listen carefully until his voice is crystal clear and you can hear the sentence you put upon that voice. Now, believe in its reality. If you will, you are living by this principle and not merely accepting the Christian faith as a substitute for living by it.

Can you imagine the turmoil which is going on in the Catholic world tonight now that the courts have cut off forty of their so-called saints? Half of my family is Catholic. I do hope that my Protestant brothers, who did not marry Catholic girls, will be big enough to mention it. I recall about twenty years ago my wife and I visited a Catholic family.

At the time my wife said to me: "They are ardent Catholics, but don't know a thing about you except that you are a Protestant and not saved." After a lovely dinner we sat around the pool and watched their three sons swim. Each boy wore a St. Christopher's medal around his neck. One was three years into the priesthood when he quit, joined the army, and returned minus his hearing. Another returned without a foot and the third minus an arm.

They told me that they believed that without this medal they would have died. Well, I wonder what will happen to that family when they learn St. Christopher never existed! The only Christ who ever existed is within you as your own wonderful human imagination. There never was another. When one being awoke to discover all that was foretold in scripture was taking place in him, he knew who the Messiah really was. He told his story, while some believed and some did not believe him.

Those who heard and believed him wrote his experiences in the form of a story, because truth is far more acceptable when told in story form, as in our four gospels. But one day we will be big enough to hear it without the story form to support us.

Redemption was foretold in the Old Testament, but not understood by those who recorded it. The prophets who prophesied the coming of the Messiah searched and inquired concerning this grace that was to be ours, and it was revealed to them that it was not for them to know. The time had not yet come, for it was for us.

Now that the horrors have been fulfilled, the Messiah who was buried in us before that the world was is beginning to erupt in the individual. Everything said of Jesus Christ will be realized in you individually, for the Bible was written about you.

Now, before the Messiah comes, you can put his word to the test. If Christ is your own wonderful human imagination and all things – be they good, bad, or indifferent – are made by him, you can imagine unlovely things and perpetuate their image.

To say that Christ makes only the good and a devil makes the evil is false, for the devil is just as phony as Christopher. When you doubt the power of Christ in you – that's the devil.

Unless you actually believe that "I am" is the being you are seeking and pray only to him by exercising your human imagination, you will never reach your desire, for awareness is the only power that can give it to you. Tonight, ask yourself what you would be aware of hearing, seeing and experiencing if your desire were now fulfilled. If what I tell you is true and your imagination is the creator of all things, then you should be able to prove his power in the testing.

I tell you: there is no intermediary between yourself and God. If you will but test this power within you, it will prove itself in performance. Then you will know who Christ really is.

Now, no one comes unto the Father except by me and I am going to tell you exactly how to come to the Father. It is not spelled out in scripture. I searched, but could not find him until he revealed himself to me. One day he will reveal himself in you, for you will see a lad, chosen by God to be his son.

The lad will be ruddy in complexion, very handsome, with beautiful eyes. He will be in his early teens. As you look into his eyes you know exactly who he is and who you are.

Then and only then do you know you are God the Father. So, no one comes to the awareness of being God the Father except by the revelation of David, for he is the one through whom you come to the awareness of Fatherhood.

In this same 14th chapter of John, Awakened Imagination asks this question: "I have been so long with you and yet you do not know me? He who has seen me has seen the Father, how then can you say, 'Show us the Father?" David is one with his father.

He is united to the Lord, having become one spirit with him. So, the only way you can ever find the Father within you is to bring forth his son, David. We are told in the 89th Psalm: "I have found David. He has cried unto me 'Thou art my Father, my God and the Rock of my salvation.'"

The word "found" recorded here, if taken on the surface implies David was lost; but the word means, "to bring forth one who is behind you." David, eternal youth, was put into the mind of man, yet so that man cannot find out what God has done from the beginning to the end when he brings forth that which was behind all along, waiting to come out. You will never know you are God the Father until David appears and calls you Father.

It is he who stated in the 2nd Psalm: "I will tell of the decree of the Lord, he said unto me, 'Thou art my son, today I have begotten thee.'" In my own case I felt an explosion in my skull, and when everything settled I saw my son leaning against the side of an open door, looking out on a pastoral scene. As he turned and looked at me standing at his right, I knew I was his father, fulfilling scripture.

The gospel is the truest story ever told but men, because of their traditions, have voided the world of God and built a stupid concept called "saints." What man on earth could be a saint? The only saints are the redeemed, those who form the body of the Risen Lord. May I tell you: everyone is predestined for that redemption.

Not one will be lost, so why pick someone out and call him a saint only to later deny he was ever a Christian? They even took Saint Nicolas off their list, claiming he never existed! Here are mortal men, without vision, appointing themselves judges of saints!

I tell you: regardless of what you do here as a mortal man you are redeemed, for redemption hasn't a thing to do with the man's ethical code. It's entirely up to the being within a man who – having played all the parts – awakens to receive the crown of righteousness which has been waiting for your return.

The moment he awakens you are redeemed. But your friends know you as mortal and have not the slightest concept of what this power is. Browning said in his "Reverie":

"From the first, Power was – I knew That, strive but for a closer view, Love were as plain to see."

This is true for: prior to power, was love. In my own case striving for love did not reveal it to me. Only when God in me unveiled himself as love was it plain to see. As love, you will exercise your almighty power in the world to come.

To have that power here, before you were incorporated into the body of love, would cause havoc in the world; for the God of whom I speak is infinite love and almighty power, and that God you are, but you will not know it until your journey is complete.

Only when he completes the journey will he unveil himself to you – his emanation – by embracing you into his own being. At that moment you will cease to be another, for you will become one with the Living God. Then you will tell your story to all who will listen.

Some will believe you and others will disbelieve, but you will tell it until you take off your mortal garment for the last time to become one with the Risen Lord who is made up of all the redeemed of humanity.

And in the end, when all are redeemed, this being who was before that the world was will be more powerful, more wise, and more glorious, because of his journey into the world of death. Learn to fine-tune your imagination.

Knowing the voice of your friend, tune him in. Determine the words you want him to say and listen carefully. Tune him in until his words are fine and clear, then believe you heard him. Think it really happened. If you will, it will come to pass.

When, I cannot say, for every imaginal act is like an egg and no two eggs (unless they are of the same species) have the same interval of time for hatching. The little bird comes out in three weeks, a sheep in five months, a horse in twelve months, and a human in nine months. Your imaginal act has its own appointed hour to ripen and flower. If it seems long, wait – for it is sure and will not be late for itself.

An imaginal act is a creative act, for the moment it is felt, the seed (or state) is fertilized. It will take a certain length of time to be born, so start today by assuming you are the man (or woman) you would like to be and let the people in your mind's eye reflect the truth of your assumption.

Be faithful to your assumption. Persist in this thought, for persistence is the way to bring your desire to pass. You don't persist through effort or fear, rather knowing that your imaginal act is now a fact; wait for its birth, for it will come.

Now, a friend wrote, saying that in her dream she was walking down the street holding a fish in her hands. The fish appeared to be dead, yet she could feel it pulse. Determine to keep the fish alive, she found a cup, filled it with water, and placed the fish inside. Then she awoke, hearing a male voice say: "Oh my darling."

Every dream contains within itself the capacity for symbolic significance. A fish is the symbol of the power of the human imagination. Imagine yourself depressed, and imagination will throw you into the pit of depression.

Imagine yourself free, and your imaginative power will bring you out, for your imagination is the savior of your world. When you become lost in the reasoning world, your imagination is not fed with your desire, for reason negates its flow. Christ, being your human imagination, is not limited by the reasoning world and all things are possible to him.

If you would ignore the facts and walk in your imaginal acts as though your wish were already fulfilled you are feeding Christ, and he becomes alive within you once more. Her dream, created by her own being who is Christ in her, was telling her she is neglecting herself.

Knowing what to do is not enough. Knowledge must be acted upon. It is so easy to accept the Christian faith and use it only as a substitute for action, and so difficult to live by it; but only as you live by your imagination can you ever know who you really are.

I had a similar experience as this lady's, but mine was in another form of the symbol of Christ, which is the pig. One night I found myself in a nursery filled with everything that grows. As I started to leave I looked down to find a little runt of a pig at my feet. Picking him up, I placed him on a table, broke off some branches of a nearby tree to cushion him, and began to search for food to feed him.

Then, as happens in dreams, the scene shifted. I am now in a vegetable market with the pig at my side. He has grown in stature but is very thin. Suddenly I realized that he was mine, so I turned to my little daughter Vicki and said: "Go get me some food that I may feed my pig." She replied: "Daddy, I don't have any money."

Then I said: "You don't need money here, for all of this belongs to us." Going over to a stand of crackers, piled in the form of a pyramid, Vicki took a box from the base, causing the entire pyramid to come tumbling down. Opening the box, I began to feed my pig when my brother Victor came by and, taking what appeared to be white, creamy grease, he spread it on my crackers saying: "This will give it sustenance."

Suddenly a lit candle appeared within the mixture and I said: "The candle is lit and it must never go out again." Then these words from scripture came to me: "His candle is lit upon my forehead and by this light I walk through darkness, for the spirit of man is the candle of the Lord."

Prior to this vision I had discovered that my imagination was the only God who ever existed, yet in spite of this discovery I had not fed it. Rather I continued to use the rational approach to life by planning my life on a reasonable basis.

Knowing of a power that did not need reason was not enough; I had to exercise this power within me. And then I was determined to exercise my imagination on behalf of myself and others. I saw my candle was lit and knew that from then on I would not let its light go out or get dim for lack of use.

Paul said: "I am a steward of the mystery." The word "steward" means "the keeper of the pig." We are told to follow the example of the dishonest steward and falsify our records. To be a steward of the mysteries, however, the pig must be fed so that you know what you are talking about. You must exercise your powerful imagination morning, noon, and night and never neglect it.

If tonight you gave a man a million dollars to invest well, he will neglect to feed his pig because to him he has it all. Then one night he will see his pig and realize what he has done to the power within him. If you are a musician and stop practicing for a week you will not be qualified to give a concert.

Only when you practice daily are you qualified. And so it is with your imagination. It must be exercised daily and then one day you will discover the Christ within you, who is God the Father, who comes only through his son David calling you Father.

CHAPTER 12

THE ONLY CHRISTIANITY

Here we believe firmly that Imagining is God; that the Supreme Power of the Universe is one with human imaging. So, when you read the Bible – a fabulous, inspired book – and you come to the word "God" you can also use the word "imagining" and you will get a clearer understanding of it.

Romans 4:20: "No distrust made him (Abraham) waver concerning the promise of God, but he grew strong in his faith as he gave glory to God, fully convinced that God was able to do what he had promised." When you read it you might think of some being external to your own Imagination.

Could you now dream of being the man or woman you want to be? That dream is a promise. We are told he was not swerved by anything in the world and gave all the glory to God, or imagining: *fully* convinced that God could do what He had promised.

If you believe what the churches teach you may think that you are not entitled to the good that you desire. (Read Romans 1:20) Ever since the creation of the world his invisible nature, namely, his eternal power and deity, has been clearly perceived in the things that have been made.

So they are without excuse; for although they knew God, they did not honor him as God or give thanks to him, but they became futile in their thinking and their senseless minds were darkened, claiming to be wise, they became fools, and exchanged the glory of the Immortal God for images resembling mortal man or birds or animals or reptiles... "and then they worshiped and served the creature rather than the Creator."

I tell you that he is speaking of this immortal being in everything that was made. Even the suit you are wearing. Someone has to first imagine it. The thing first imagined is the invisible image and then it becomes externalized as a hat or a suit or a house.

Today a friend called me concerning a personal problem. She said, "You said your father has objective vision. He could see the images of his imagining as real as the forms of Nature." I knew this is true. The whole vast world that he built for his ten children, he built out of his wonderful imagination.

He would sit alone and conjure before him men and women and see situations as he wanted to see them. And then he would arrest that state just before sleep and he controlled it completely. And when he later returned to his offices and these things came to pass, he was not surprised. Others set the deals in motion that he had already seen in his mind's eye.

This lady called to tell me about her sister's husband. Her father had opposed the marriage and had said that this man would never be any good, and he had set forth in detail just what he would do. He said, "He will father your child but he will not support it. He will live in a bar and he will always be worthless."

This man has fulfilled that prophesy in every detail. Her father was a powerful figure in the theater and disliked his son-in-law and prophesied his future and it has come true in detail. I told this lady a story about a prophesy of my father's years ago.

In 1919 at the turn of the year, I can see my father at the head of the table and all of us children sitting there and he said to my mother, "There will be a war in 20 years, Wilsey. It will be in the fall. Germany will again be at war with England. Japan will be in it, and Russia and Italy. America will be our great ally."

My mother looked around the table at her sons and said, "My boys will be of the age to go to that war. What are you talking about? He said, "It will be true and already all the ships are discussing it." He was a ship's chandler and talked with many people. My father did not know that this power he had of imagining as God.

He could take a man or woman or a community and see them so vividly in imagining in his own living room that they became objective to him, and afterwards find them coming to his office to propose what he had inwardly set in motion. But he did not identify that power that creates his world with this supreme power that he called God. "Ever since the creation of the world his invisible nature, his eternal power, has been clearly perceived in the things that have been made."

My father saw everything as made. He discussed a program with a man and afterward the man comes to him and proposes the deal that my father had already closed in his imagination. But he did not identify it with God. "They exchanged the glory of the immortal God for images resembling mortal man... and served the creature rather than the Creator."

Everyone here – your invisible presence is God, but if you imagine money into being and you make a million, suddenly you worship the million, not the power that made it possible. You enter a certain social circle and then you forget that you brought it into being by imagining and now you think this group is what is all-important.

So man forgets and exchanges the glory of the immortal God for the image of a mortal man or something that vanishes. For everything visible will vanish; but you will not vanish. Even this great land will one day be washed by the sea but you will not be. That which brought things into being cannot cease to be. So we are warned.

I told this lady about my father and she said. "Your father did that in 1919, but I will go back to 1919, and my father said, "I do not want to buy a paper because I can see the headlines and they say WAR!" He was so determined and convinced that he would not buy one for weeks, and when he did finally buy it, the headline said, WAR!

Then the lady asked if her father's attitude towards the sister's husband had determined what happened, and whether she should continue helping her sister who was always in need. Yes, it determined what happened. But now it could be changed radically. Give to the sister if she needs help. But then I told her that this power is all imagining and it is one tissue with our own wonderful imagination.

There is only ONE. We do not differ in nature or substance from IT but only in degree of intensity. If we could imagine anything in the world and not swerve and not turn and give all glory to this power called God, nothing could keep it from coming into being.

God speaks to man through the language of dreams, but I do not have to go to sleep to dream. I can imagine something for you and desire it with all my heart. If I imagine something for another, that is God speaking to me. I do not have to see a face.

There is such difference between what the churches call God and what the mystic knows is God. Blake speaks of Christianity in the last chapter of his great work "Jerusalem." He breaks it into four chapters, like the four rivers, etc., and he tells us: "I give you the end of a golden string, Only wind it into a ball: It will lead you in at Heaven's gate, Built in Jerusalem's wall."

And then he defines Christianity. *Articles of Faith?* He completely discounts them. He says:

"I know of no other Christianity and of no other Gospel than the liberty of both body and mind to exercise the Divine Arts of Imagination. Imagination, the real and eternal World of which this Vegetable Universe is but a faint shadow, and in which we shall live in our eternal or Imaginative Bodies when these Vegetable Mortal Bodies are no more."

No other Christianity than the right to exercise the divine arts of Imagination. So I say to you, "I would like so and so. I am too close to the picture, so would you now exercise the divine art and hear so and so for me?" And you say to me, "Will you hear something for me? Imagine you have told me that what you want is now so, and give all the glory to the power that creates in this world."

I have personally done this unnumbered times. It is the only Christianity in the world. It has nothing to do with any church. The only Christianity is the liberty to exercise the divine arts of Imagination. Can I do it? Who is doing it? God is doing it! I do not have to make any form.

The supreme power of the universe is one with human Imagination. If we go back to the Old Testament and take the word "maker," it means Imagination. "Your maker is your husband, the Lord of Hosts is his name."

The word "Potter" means Imagination. "I went down to the potter's house and he was working at his wheel, and the vessel in his hand was spoiled, but he worked it into another vessel such as seemed good to him."

If I would only take that and use the word "Imagination," but the translator could not bring himself to use it. What is in my mental hand that I am making? If it is not good and I do not revise it, then I am turning my wheel and recreating that same picture, but if I am a wise potter I will change it and hear you tell me that you now have what you desire.

I will make a new vessel. Who is doing it? The potter – and that is imagination. All day long I think the same thing over and over. I am working at the wheel of recurrence. Everyone here can be the man or woman they want to be. I know it from my own family. Have you ever noticed how if you go into a business and take all the facts and estimate just how things will come out, how often they come about as you said. Who did it? You are not a prophet, but you are imagining, and the state then comes true.

Not a thing is brought into being by any power outside itself. It is sustained by the activity of the one who brought it into being. So, if I brought in poverty it can only remain as long as I am conscious of being poor. The moment I cease to imagine that I am poor then things begin to change.

There was a play on Broadway called, "The Million-airess," and a critic wrote sarcastically that Kathryn Hepburn was trying to impress us with the fact that all a pauper needs to become rich is the arrogance of wealth. He was wiser than he knew! The arrogance of wealth is all he needs to stop being a pauper.

You walk in a state and it is an activity of mind and to the degree you can sustain it, to that degree you will create it. The whole world is nothing but God and God is Imagining and man is Imagination and "We dwell in him and he in us, and we are one." Now you try it. You take something tonight. If you are too close to your own picture, do it for someone else and see that one as he would like to be seen by himself and then remain faithful to it. He may never know you did it for him, but that doesn't matter.

When the thing happens so naturally that he will never think that what you did was responsible. He has exchanged the glory of God for an image resembling mortal man. He will say he met a certain person and they influenced someone else, or recommended him, and that brought it all to pass. These things get the credit and he forgets immortal God.

I have told you the story before of a friend who came to me because he desperately needed a larger income, etc., to care for the educational needs of his family. His present bank position held no hope of advancement. I taught him what to do and while I was absent in Barbados he did it and when I returned, he told me he had secured this fabulous position with the Rockefeller Foundation, where he still is.

But as time went on, he is so literal minded, that he began to forget how it came about and now he gives full credit to the man who spoke to him in church and finally asked him to come into the Foundation. This man is now a powerful person in my friend's mind and is the cause of his good fortune. He has transferred the glory that belongs to God to the image of a man.

No matter what you are doing, can you see clearly what you want to do and carry on a conversation inwardly with a friend which will imply that which you desire is now a fact? Then do it. For on higher levels of Imagining inner activity is revealed by inner conversation.

If man would listen to what he is inwardly saying, he would know what he is setting in motion. As man walks the street if he would pause and say "what am I saying now?" he would find that 99% are justifying failure. But we are told, "You are without excuse for you have seen him and his work, yet you deny it."

When you hear the word God or Jesus Christ you think of some being external to your own imagining, but there is none for Imagining is God. That is what lights every being in the world, and as you imagine, so you will become.

So no matter what your present limitations are, you can start now to dream the most noble dream, and you can walk through this door tonight as though it is true knowing that your Imagining is God. There is no fiction. You can write your own novel and realize it. Even someone in a dungeon may be imagining and who knows what he may call forth.

If I were in a dungeon I would move the world if necessary to get out. A body may be physically confined, but you cannot confine God. Man only sees the proximate cause; the real cause of something you cannot see; for the invisible power is what is creating.

Who knows who may convulse the world. It may even be a woman "treading" in the wine press. Everyone here, you can be what you want to be, no matter what your dream is, if you are willing to let God do it, God being your own Imagining. You walk completely suspended above appearances and you will become what you desire.

This is the only Christianity I know – the freedom to exercise this divine art of Imagining. Now you try it. If you are here for the first time I challenge you to disprove it. Everyone has the same power. Because one has a million does not make him any more a creator than you are.

Be careful what you are imagining for what you are Imagining you will create, though it may convulse the world. I hope you have the Revised Version of the Bible for it is from what I have quoted tonight. It is more accurate in meaning if not as orally beautiful as the King James Version.

You will find in Romans that recreation for it all, for after Acts Paul lays the foundation and he states, "I am a child of Abraham and one of the tribe of Benjamin. But he sees it now not as the code but the spirit, and he sees circumcision no longer as only a physical act.

He realizes that he is now a true Christian. He did not go to any church. He sees now the spirit of the law and not the letter. You cannot be born a Christian! It is a way of life that you adopt.

You could be born in the Vatican with the Pope as your father and you would not be a Christian. You can only be a Christian when you see the reality and adopt it as a way of life. The law was given to man but they break through from the letter of the law and find the spirit of it and live by it, and that is Christianity.

There are many religions based on many 'isms" but that is not Christianity. It is the liberty of body and mind to exercise the divine arts of Imagination. This lady can change the picture for her sister's husband. She can imagine that he is now generous, because now he has so much that he wants to give to her as she gave to him, and she can break the spell cast on him.

I know my mother when she darned our socks dreamed for each of us of a future of which she would be proud. Everyone of us is living a noble life and I know she dreamed it for all of us. She never spared her shoe, wham! If you did something wrong.

She left the world with her dream fixed in her mind and it came true. We can dream for ourselves or for our neighbors and that dream is the voice of God, for God speaks to man through the medium of a dream.

CHAPTER 13

BONUS: FULFILLMENT OF GODS PLAN

I think you're all aware that this is the most dramatic week in Christendom and yet I dare say that not half of one percent of those who call themselves Christians really understand what it is all about. It's the story of the fulfillment of God's purpose.

That's the week, the triumphant march into Jerusalem, the crucifixion and then the resurrection. And it's told as though it took place on earth.

That's how the story is told. For as Tennyson said, "Truth embodied in a tale shall enter in at lowly doors." So, man cannot think abstractly so it's told in the form of a story. And man has mistaken the story for the reality. Let us now look to see who the one is spoken of in scripture. They say his name is Jesus. You may not believe me but I'll tell you who Jesus is.

Say, "I Am," that's Jesus. Don't say, I am man or John or Peter or anything, just I Am. That's Jesus. That's God. That's the Lord God Jehovah. The crucifixion is already over. It was in the beginning of time, a deliberate act on the part of God – all over. The resurrection took place and is taking place and will continue until everyone is awake. So, you say, "I Am," that's Jesus.

Now, it begins with the march. Mark tells us that He took the twelve and then He walked ahead of them. The way Mark states it, it is as if he were one whom a dream had possessed and who went forward to fulfill all that the prophets had foretold.

For he said, "I have come to fulfill scripture." The only purpose. Now, not a man on the outside fulfilling scripture. This one, which is God, is buried in you when you say, "I am." You may not be aware of it aside from dreaming the dream of life which is this. He also is dreaming the fulfillment of His purpose.

And the day will come, you are going to reproduce within yourself all that is said in scripture concerning Jesus. Then you will know who Jesus is.

It is said that he told them, "we're going up to Jerusalem, and all that was written of the son of man by the prophets will be accomplished." And the evangelist adds, "They understood none of these things." This saying was hid from them and they did not grasp what was said.

Only the Risen Lord can interpret scripture. Only His finger could trace the ambiguous phrases of scripture and extract their heavenly meaning. It's a pattern in scripture. That only when He rises in you as you, can you take the Old Testament and simply follow the pattern.

You know what the pattern is because you've experienced it. And the whole thing unfolds and the whole thing is told you in the Old Testament. But it's a pattern.

It's told you as though it's history, ancient history. It's divine history and that history, not page after page, but a pattern goes through the entire thing and then that pattern unfolds within you. And when it unfolds within you, you actually gain that certainty that, "I Am He." There is no other way you'll ever know it until it unfolds within you.

Now, God came and comes into human history. And now we're going to give Him a name – in the person of Jesus, but the Jesus in you, in me, in every child born of woman. That's the only Jesus in eternity. I Am that Jesus. Well, now He's a father. When God is born within you, for that's the beginning of it all, you first awaken within you and you do not know you are God.

You only know that you have awakened from the most profound sleep ever and it seemed like eternity. You did not awake on the bed where you fell asleep the night before. You awoke in a tomb and the tomb is your skull. And you awake within your skull and you're all alone with no one present. But you have a built-in innate knowledge what to do.

And you do it and you come out of your skull as a child comes out of the womb of woman. But you're coming out of your own skull and you pull yourself out of your own skull. And the imagery of scripture concerning the birth of God surrounds you, including the little babe wrapped in swaddling clothes and three witnesses to the event. So, you're told, "When they came, they saw the heavenly being but Him they did not see." It's the birth of God. God actually took upon Himself the limit of contraction, which is man. Now He is born, the birth being an expansion.

There is no limit to expansion. God is forever expanding and then, at a moment of expansion, He
then has a new venture of contraction. Then He expands beyond what He was. Then He contracts.
Then He expands beyond what He was and that is
God's play. There is no limit to expansion. He puts a
limit to contraction. The limit is man.

So, when you break the tomb, you come out and you
are God. Therefore, no one can see you. The heavenly hosts who were present to witness the event
can't see you, for you are spirit; you are God. But
you see them and you see the babe and you see
everything round about you just as described in
Luke and Matthew. But you do not know that you
are God.

That comes later, and you'll not in eternity know
you are God until God's son calls you Father. And
God's son, the Christ of Scripture, is not Jesus. It's
David. Jesus is the Lord. Jesus is the Lord God Jehovah in you when you say, "I Am." That's Jesus.
That's not David. Who then is Christ? The Son of
God. David then comes and when David comes,
there is no uncertainty as to who you are. For he
calls you Father.

And before he utters the word Father, you know you
are his Father. And he knows he is your son. And

this relationship is now what every heart is aching for. When this is established by an actual experience, the drama is over. Everything is over that you came to perform – to find the son who, in turn, will reveal you as God the Father. For He is sound asleep in humanity and man doesn't know that he is God.

And when he is born from above, he still doesn't know he is God. And not in eternity can he find out who he is until the son appears. So, we are told in Scripture:

"No one knows who the son is except the Father and no one knows who the Father is except the Son and anyone to whom He chooses to reveal Him."

So, hey do it because "They know neither my Father nor Me. Had they known my Father, they would have known me also. But they know neither My Father nor Me."

So, you find, you've got to actually feel between the words. For He's speaking one moment as Father and then speaking, in another moment as Son. It's a mystery and how are you going to tell it unless you tell it in the form of a story that it may enter in at lowly doors.

But man, hearing the story, learns to feel behind the story and feel what it's trying to convey. But when you actually experience the story, then you know the mystery. It's the mystery that everyone one day will unfold within himself and he'll know that he is God. So this is what confronts man this week as it's dramatized but not told. For they do not know it.

They do not know the story. Let me turn now to the 55th Chapter of Isaiah. "I will make a covenant with you." Now he's speaking to all of us, "I will make a covenant with you," and this is his covenant, "my steadfast, sure love for David – I have made him a witness to the peoples."

That is my witness to the peoples. Now what is he going to witness? The truth of God's word. So God's word is Scripture and the Scripture spoken of was the Old Testament, "and the word is truth," I make him now a witness to the people and He has my steadfast and sure love forever.

Now, "That is my covenant with you," said the Lord to us. We turn now to the trial, and here we find one called Jesus standing before Pilot, and he turns to Pilot and he said, "For this I was born. And for this I came into the world to bear witness to the truth."

Now He tells you He is not of this world, "unless you are born form above, you cannot enter the Kingdom of Heaven." He's not speaking of the birth from the womb of a woman in spite of all the priest-hoods of the world. He is speaking of an entirely different birth, "born not of blood nor of the will of the flesh, nor of the will of man, but of God." He said, "I am from above, you are from below."

Now, He's not speaking to you, the being who is God. He is speaking to this body here. This is from below. This came out of the womb of my mother. But there is that in me which is "I Am" that no woman can bear. That must be born from above. It is now entombed in my skull, entombed in your skull. But the skull of which I speak is a divine skull containing all of us.

That is the skull. And it is said in the 87th Psalm, "And this one was born here and that one was born there." All within the one grand skull and it's called Zion – another name for Jerusalem. So, when Paul said, "The Jerusalem from above is our mother and she bears children into liberty." The Jerusalem from below bears them into slavery.

Well, my physical mother bearing her ten children that she raised, she wove garments of flesh. And these garments of flesh came from below, from her womb into slavery. For we're all slaves of the bodies that we wear.

But housed within that, from above, there is another Jerusalem and she is our mother who bears us
into liberty, into freedom. You come out of your
own skull, that divine skull. And you're set free.
Well, then you come into this world to bear witness
to what? To the truth. So, "I made him a witness to
all the peoples."

Well, what is he going to witness now? The truth of
Scripture, that God is a Father and that He did say
to me, "I will tell of the decree of the lord," said
David in the 2nd Psalm. "He said unto me, thou art
my Son. Today I have begotten thee." If Scripture
cannot be broken, what other Son are you holding
up now before me that I may see?

You may see all the hallucinations in the world as
artists have painted dozens and dozens of different
portraits of one they call Jesus. And they said they
saw him. Ask the artist, "When you saw him in your
imagination and you painted on the canvas or you
sculpted, did you know then you're looking at the
Son of God." If they say, "yes," well then you must
know that you are God. Because no one can see the
Son but the Father and no one knows the Son but
the Father.

Therefore, if you are looking at the Son of God and
only God can see the Son, well then you must be

God. What are they going to say to that? And Scripture cannot be broken. Read it in the 11th Chapter of the Book of Matthew. "No one knows who the Son is except the Father and no one knows who the Father is except the Son and anyone to whom He chooses to reveal Him.

So, I know in my own case, raised in the Christian faith as I was, and I call myself a Christian from my own personal experience of this great mystery, but I did not know from my mother's knee or in my school (because we had Bible reading and Bible study when I was a child, it was part of our schooling). We had to go to Sunday School. I was taught the Bible, raised with the Bible.

And there it is but I didn't see it and my teachers didn't see it. My mother didn't see it; my father didn't see it, and no one that I ever met ever saw it, so I didn't know it until it happened. It happened in me and then I could not then make it fit in with what they taught me.

I had to go back and re-read Scripture and there the whole pattern was there all along but only the Risen Christ can interpret Scripture. Only when David rises within me and calls me Father.

Now, listen to the words, "When the time had fully come, God sent forth the spirit of his Son into our hearts crying Father." What time has fully come? When you have borne the great fardel, the great load, the burden the allotted span.

Not before you've borne it the allotted span can He come. And when you get to the end of the road and you've borne that burden, then the spirit of His Son comes into you and here he rises in you.

You resurrect your own son and that son is God's Son; therefore, you are God. That's when you gain the certainty that you are God. Yet, while you wear the little garment, you are still in a straight jacket. And all you can do while you wear it is to tell it.

Try to clarify the atmosphere and scrape off the barnacles from the ship that gathers them over the centuries. Far from belittling Jesus, I have placed Him where He actually is. He is God. He is not the Son of God. He is God.

He is the Lord, a symbol of God, that you may say, but He wasn't born of any woman. The only woman of whom He was born, "I Am."

That's the Jerusalem from above. "I am Mary and birth to Christ must give if I in blessedness for now and ever more would live." So each must bring forth the Son and it's the same Son. Only one Son.

And when you look at Him, no uncertainty; no one need tell you anything. There you are, looking at your Son as though memory has now returned and you have suffered from total amnesia up to this moment in time and suddenly, your memory returns and you know who you are.

You're God, the Father. It's going to happen to every child born of woman. Not one will be lost. Not one.

I don't care if you're a moron today, if you're brainless. That's only a temporary experience in this world. That brain that you have really, the true brain, is not really addled at all. That's only some distorted aspect of life for a little while.

Maybe you'll go through life, spending fifty, sixty years in some distorted brain, but it's still not the brain of which I speak. Not that divine brain. If your child is not a balanced child, a demented child, I know it's a hard thing to bring up and a hard thing to face in life, but that's not your responsibility.

That little thing there that you call your child that is demented, behind it all, behind that mask it is part of the burden that it bears, is the perfect being that is Jesus and that Jesus in there is, "I Am." It was never tarnished.

It was never soiled, no matter what it has done in the world, it was never soiled. And one day, it will awake. And when it awakes, it comes out of the tomb.

So Paul could say, "I am crucified with Christ; nevertheless I live, not I. Christ lives in me and the life I now live in the flesh, I live by faith in the Son of God who loved me and gave Himself for me." And that Son is David.

Listen to the words, "I have found in David, the Son of Jesse, a man after my own heart who will do all my will." Well, the word "Jesse" means "Jehovah exists." That's what the word means. So Jesse is the Father. Whose Father? David's Father. And who is Jesse? Jehovah. And who is Jesus? Jehovah. He is the Lord.

But no one can say Jesus is Lord except by the Holy Spirit. And who is the Holy Spirit? *The remembrance.* When the Son stands before you and memory returns and you are his Father and He is your Son, then only by this return of memory will you ever know.

And so, no one can say that Jesus is Lord and Jesus is the Father. For in spirit, David called him, "my Lord." Why did he call him, my Lord? Well, that's a title of Father.

So he called Jesus, My Lord. He is the I Am in you, the I Am in every being in this world. So, we'll go up to Jerusalem and all that was actually written about the son of man, which is the title that he used of self, will now be accomplished. So, I'm going up to Jerusalem, because everything is going to happen in the skull. That's where Jerusalem is, the Jerusalem above.

I'm going up to Jerusalem, not down. And all things said of the Son of man will now be accomplished. So, he goes up and the whole thing unfolds within the skull. That's where you awake. That's where you explode.

When David comes out, it's an explosion in your head as though you had put some dynamite to your head and the whole thing explodes. And when it all settles, here stands David before you.

He was buried in you. And when he said to me, "I laid myself down within you to sleep," who said that? The depths of my own soul, the Lord said that. "I laid myself down within you to sleep and as I slept I dreamed a dream. I dreamed, and I knew exactly what he was dreaming.

He's dreaming that He's I. And when the dream is over, we aren't two. We are one. No longer will he simply treat me as something on the outside, an emanation of His. No more the emanation, He cleaves to me and we become one being.

So when a man leaves this world, his father, his mother, and cleaves to his wife, and this is the wife, the emanation of God. Yet, though His emanation, it's his wife until the dream is over. When the sleep is over, we aren't two. We're one.

And I know that when I awoke within me, I wondered, "How did I get here? Who put me here?" For this is a tomb. This s a sepulcher and only one who thought me dead could have put me here. For this is a tomb and only the dead are placed in tombs. So someone, I didn't realize then, that it was a deliberate act on my own part.

So, you're told in the 10th Chapter of John, "No one takes away my life, I lay it down myself. I have the power to lay it down and the power to take it up again." And yet, over the centuries, we have condemned a race of people for taking away the life of one who never, as an individual, walked the face of this earth.

He is in man or you couldn't even breathe. He's not on the outside of man that someone can take his life. He is in man. He's the breath of man, the spirit of man, the I Amness of man, man's own wonderful human imagination.

That is Jesus. That's God. And so to blame a race of people for doing what no one ever did, listen to the

Bible, the 10th Chapter, "No one takes away my life. I lay it down myself. I have the power to lay it down and the power to take it up again. For I am the resurrection and the life." So he entered death's door, the human skull, and laid down in the grave of man and there he dreams the dream of life, and this is the dream of life.

And one day, it comes to the end and he awakes. Where? In the tomb where he entered to find himself there. It was a long dream, thousands and thousands of years he has been dreaming this dream. You didn't begin in your mother's womb seventy years ago or whatever year you may be. That's only a garment woven for you.

You are eternal. You have no beginning and you have no end. Never was there a time when you were not. Nor shall there ever come a time when you shall cease to be.

Beginnings and ends are all dreams. It seems so real, but they're all dreams. But you have no beginning, no end. You are and that being is called in Scripture, God the Father. But, may I tell you something?

You will not actually feel that "I am Jesus; I am the Father." That's not what you feel. You don't feel Jesus. You don't feel God. You don't feel Jehovah.

These are names given by man. But what you do feel is Father.

So the great revelation of the New Testament is God is Father. That is the foundation of the entire thing. If you were not a father, then there is no child. So the relationship of father & son is fundamental to the Christian faith.

Without the Son, there would not be a Father. And if there is a Father, there must be a Son. And it's a search for the Son. And when the Son is found, the Father knows who He is. But not until the Son is resurrected. So, in the Old Testament, in the 2nd Psalm, the 16th Psalm, and the 110th Psalm, they are identified with resurrection.

In the 16th Psalm, David is speaking and is made to say, "Thou wouldst not leave my soul in Hell." In confidence, he knows he would not be left in Hell, that he would be raised up. Because, "I will not take my steadfast, sure love from David." That's my covenant with the peoples.

I have made him a witness to all the peoples. I will not take my love from him. So, he dies and is buried but I will raise him up. And when the Father raises up the Son then the smile is on his face because his Son has returned from the grave.

And David is the eternal Son of God, the resultant state of all the experiences that you, as a man, which is God as man, experience in this world. So God became as I am that I may be as He is.

This is the story of scripture and it's all in the Old Testament but not understood. There it is, a blueprint. It's an adumbration. The New interprets the Old, not the other way around. And when it happens in you, well, what a joy. I can't tell anyone the emotion that possesses you and then you really are like one possessed.

You walk in the dream of what happened and you can't think of anything but, really. You may be diverted for a little while, a small party. A big one would bore you. A few friends, yes. A large crowd, no. It doesn't interest you.

A dinner party of a few chosen friends, yes. But to have an enormous crowd, no that's nothing more than noise. Everyone is trying to, well, monopolize the entire picture. But a few chosen friends for a party, a delightful evening with words where you are discussing reality, wonderful.

But after it happens to you, may I tell you, you can't think of anything but. And your dreams are not dreams any more. Your nights are not what they were prior to that waking. You wake and it's entirely different. And I can't explain to anyone who wakes every day of their life after a night of good sleep, that that waking in the morning doesn't compare to this.

It's something entirely different, as though you had never awakened before in your life. That's what actually you feel like. Something entirely different. And you look at all these things round about you and here, a thousand years, two thousand years, three thousand years ago, it was written there and it was all about you, and you didn't know it.

So we're going to go up now to Jerusalem, said he, "and all that is written of the Son of man by the prophets will be fulfilled." All will be accomplished. Then he began to explain to them Scripture and said, "Beginning with Moses and the Law and all the prophets and the Psalms, he interpreted to them in all the Scriptures, the things concerning Himself."

Now this coming Friday, if you do go to part of the service, you will hear the words on the cross. Every one is taken from the Old Testament. And you will know who you are in that sense. They are the words of David. For David is going to commit himself now to his Father. "Into thy hands, I commit my spirit." This is now the 31st Psalm.

"Thou hast redeemed me, Oh Lord, Faithful God," yet that is the final cry on the cross when you read it in this little Book of Luke. "Into thy hands I commit my spirit." And he commits it into the hands of the Father. He calls him now Father, "Father, into thy hands I commit my spirit." And these are the identical words of David in the 31st Psalm.

Now here, the entire thing unfolds within man. But, something was said to me just before I took the platform by a very dear friend of mine who is here tonight although he will admit to me and to everyone in the world, he is one hundred and one percent American but he cannot deny the fact that he has one hundred and one percent of the Irish background in him too.

So, he gave me the definition of an Irishman. An Irishman is one who does not know what he wants and there will be no peace on earth until he finds it. Not exactly his words; he told it much better than that, but that's the essence of it. He does not know what he wants and there will be no peace on earth until he finds it.

Well, that's the whole vast world. Ask, what do you want. He doesn't really know what he wants because what everyone wants is to find the Father and you can't find the Father without the Son. Basically, we're trying to find the cause of the phenomenon of life.

What makes things happen in my world? He told me, "You know, years ago," before he met me, "he had these sorts of daydreams of, well, talking to a crowd – maybe going on radio, maybe on TV." Here out of the blue, someone came into his restaurant in Ojai and offered him a series of lectures here, in New Mexico, possibly sending him into Arizona.

She can arrange other things for him, and the whole thing is done. But he remembered these daydreams. Most of us don't remember and when we are confronted with our own harvest, we deny it's our harvest. So, I tell you there is no such thing as an accident in this world. No. There is no such thing as a natural cause.

Every natural effect has a spiritual cause, that is, an imaginal cause and not a natural. A natural only seems. It is a delusion of our fading memory. We can't remember when we set it in motion. He remembers that long before he met me in San Francisco, that this happened back East, this daydream of his.

And now, suddenly out of the nowhere a seeming stranger comes into his world, listening to him in his restaurant, carried away with what he had to say and the way he said it and is moved to arrange this thing for him. He doesn't have to lift a finger to do it. It all will be done for him.

So, I say, dream noble dreams, wonderful dreams. If they don't come to pass tonight, tomorrow, or next week, you keep on dreaming them. But try to put yourself into the dream as though it's taking place and try to live in it.

Be possessed by the dream and see the whole thing unfold within you in this world of Caesar, always bearing in mind, the real dream. It must come to an end only when it's fulfilled. And the story is the fulfillment when you awake. For resurrection is waking. It's not gathering dead bones together and putting flesh on it. It's simply awakening.

You are sound asleep and you awaken like a man out of a deep, deep sleep to find yourself in a tomb. But you have the strength to break the bonds of that tomb and to come out of that tomb. And when they come to search for the body, they have taken away the body.

They only knew you by reason of the body that you wore and that's taken away and they can't see you. "Him they could not see." But he was fully aware of everyone round about him. And, here, all the symbolism of Scripture is unfolding before him.

And he is the central character in the entire drama. They're talking about him. They aren't talking about Jesus. They're talking about you. You are individualized and you tend forever and forever toward ever greater individualization. They didn't call me by any other name. They didn't call me God. Didn't call me Lord, didn't call me Jesus.

They spoke of me as Neville. It's Neville's baby. I was aware of being "I." No loss of identify whatsoever. But then when David comes, here is Neville.

In this century I was born, the year 1905. Here we have a recorded, so-called history, of one born 1000 years BIC. and he stands before me and I know I'm his father. And here we have words put into his mouth that the Lord said to him, 'You are my son." And I know that I am his Father and only then did I gain the certainty as to whom I am.

So, you will not lose your identity, yet you are God the Father. It is Father that is being revealed, the sweetest name there is in Scripture.

He is a loving Father, may I tell you, in spite of all the pain you've gone through and all the horrors of the world. For this is a nightmare. Can't confine it only to the night; it's a daymare too with most people.

So, I tell you, at the end – it's not a reward – it's simply victory. You have plotted and planned the whole thing before you entered the tomb. You prepared a way for your own return to whom? To yourself.

I came out from the Father and I came into the world. Again, I am leaving the world and I'm returning to the father. And that's the story of this week. So as far as Friday goes, Good Friday, save your tears. The crucifixion is over. And it was a voluntary act on your part, which is God's part.

You laid yourself down in a tomb for the purpose of dreaming the dream of life. And in that dream, you suffered. You knew you would. As you're told in the 24th Chapter of the Book of Luke, again you're told it in the 18th, for that matter. But the 24th,"Oh foolish men and slow of heart to understand all that the prophets have written and said about the Christ.

Was it not necessary that Christ suffer these things and then enter into his glory." It's part of the training. These are the furnaces. "I tried you in the furnaces of affliction." Why? For my own sake. "For my own sake I do it, for how should my name be profaned. My glory I will not give to another."

And my name is Father. That's my name. That's my name. That's the name truly that is God's name in the world. And so the word "God" which makes the mind jump on the outside is not truly the name.

You take the word "Eloheim" and we translate it "God." Take the word, "Jod He Vau He" and translate that "Lord." But the name that is revealed is Father. That's who this being is. This creative being is Father. And everyone is in search of the Father.

And one day, He's going to find the only one who can reveal Him as Father. And when He finds Him, He finds His own Son David. Now that will come as an awful shock to the majority of people in the world. And I would not take back one little iota.

It's true. I'm not speculating. I'm telling you exactly what I have experienced. It's not theory with me. This is all that I know from my own personal experience. It was always there in that Book called the Bible but I had not experienced it so I couldn't see it.

"You have eyes and you see not. And you have ears and you hear not." Because they're not yet bored. And it takes the furnaces to bore these eyes for you and to bore the mouth for you, to bore the ears for you that you may experience Scripture and then the whole thing unfolds within you.

It's all about you because it's all about God and you are God asleep. And the day is coming and may it not be too long when He will awake in you as you. And then you will find your Son that Scripture claims to be God's Son. And because Scripture claims it is God's Son and you know it's your Son, then you must be God.

That's the story of the Bible.

GLOSSARY OF CITED VERSES

(In chronological order)
Luke 18:31-34
Matthew 27:46
Mark 15:34
Psalms 22:1
John 19:20
Luke 23:46
Psalm 31:5
Romans 6:5
Genesis 17:19
Isaiah 14:24
Philippians 1:6
John 12:24
Isaiah 48:10,11
Luke 23:33
Hebrews 5:6
Luke 18:34
Psalm 2:7
Eccl. 3:11
I Samuel 17:2.5
Proverbs 16:4
Job 42:5
John 14:29
Isaiah 6:2
Isaiah 49:5
Isaiah 11:1-3
Jeremiah 23:5
Zechariah 3:8
Zechariah 6:12

Isaiah 4:2
Matthew 1:17
Isaiah 11:1-3
Isaiah 55:11
Romans 6:5
II Corinthians 3:6
II Timothy 2:18
Deuteronomy 34
Psalm 22
Acts 9:20
Matthew 5:17
Luke 22:37
Luke 24:27
Psalm 40:8
Acts 13:22
John 8:36
I Samuel 16:12-13
John 1:13
Luke 15:32
Matthew 5:48
Luke 1:37
Matthew 11:27
Luke 10:22
Matthew 22:43
Psalm 89:26
I Corinthians 12:8-10
I Corinthians 13:15
Psalm 2:7
John 17:4,5
I Corinthians 1:21
Romans 8:39
I Corinthians 4:7
Psalm 40:7,8
Galatians 2:19,20
II Timothy 4

Romans 4:20
Romans 1:20
Isaiah 55
Psalm 87
John 10
Psalm 31

ABOUT THE AUTHOR

Neville Lancelot Goddard (1905–1972), was a New Thought pioneer, lecturer, and mystic who wrote on the Bible, esotericism and is considered to be a founder of the "law of assumption".

Goddard was born in Barbados on February 19, 1905 to Joseph Nathaniel and Wilhelmina Goddard. He emigrated to New York City in the 1920s, where he first worked as a professional dancer.

In 1931, Neville began to study under an Ethiopian rabbi who introduced him to the Kabbalah. After a brief stint in the Army, he officially became a United States citizen. In the 1950s, Goddard lectured at The Town Hall on the many religious topics which served as the source of this book.

Neville's legacy includes greatly inspiring great minds like Rhonda Byrne and Wayne Dyer, as well as Carlos Castaneda.

www.ingramcontent.com/pod-product-compliance
Lightning Source LLC
Chambersburg PA
CBHW011220120626
46545CB00010B/3082